To Bert 1999

BEGIN BRIDGE

G. C. H. Fox

RIGHT WAY

Printed and bound in Great Britain by Cox & Wyman Ltd., Reading, Berkshire.

The *Right Way* series and the *Paperfronts* series are both published by Elliot Right Way Books, Brighton Road, Lower Kingswood, Tadworth, Surrey, KT20 6TD, U.K.

CONTENTS

PREFACE

This book is written for the complete beginner in bridge. I have assumed that the reader has no knowledge of bridge, or indeed of any card game. The first part describes in the simplest language how the game is played, its object and the elements of scoring.

Part 2 is devoted to the bidding. There are several methods or systems of bidding and it is impossible in the space of this book to describe them all. Therefore, I have concentrated on the methods most popular in Great Britain. Although these may differ in some particulars from the methods favoured elsewhere, such as in America, much of the fundamental framework of bidding is the same the world over and is based on common sense.

Parts 3 and 4 deal with the defenders' game and the play of the hand by declarer.

Throughout this book I have endeavoured to provide good reasons for everything that I have advised. Long experience in teaching has proved repeatedly that to confront beginners with so-called rules is a mistake. Provide guiding principles backed up by reasons, certainly. But to dish out rules as if they were local government regulations can never assist a beginner to master the game of bridge.

I have devoted more space to the strong no trump than the weak.

The majority of those attending bridge classes for beginners are middle-aged or retired folk who want to learn so that they can play social bridge with their friends.

Although later they may advance to playing duplicate bridge, I am more concerned with the skills necessary for social rubber bridge. Most social players play the strong no trump. However, classes conducted by qualified English Bridge Union instructors are usually told to play the weak no trump. This is because the English Bridge Union is keen to recruit new members who will play duplicate bridge at their clubs, where the weak no trump nowadays finds itself virtually taken for granted.

Nonetheless, to play the strong no trump is not necessarily the hallmark of a beginner. Nor is it (as it has been described) 'only for the elderly and golf club players'. On the contrary, it is played by leading American and continental players and they do not do too badly in international championships.

While I consider the strong no trump is certainly the most practical method for those who play mainly social rubber bridge, it is clearly right to learn both the strong and the weak no trump.

G.C.H. Fox

PART ONE

INTRODUCTORY AND HOW THE GAME IS PLAYED

Contract Bridge is a game for four players, two of whom sit opposite one another and play as partners against the other two. Throughout this book we shall refer to the players, for convenience, by the terms North, South, East and West. So in the diagram below North and South (N & S) are playing against East and West (E & W).

The Pack

The game is played with one pack of fifty-two cards (no jokers) and the cards rank in the order of ace (highest), followed by king, queen, etc., down to the two (lowest).

There are four suits; these are, in their ranking order, Spades ♠, Hearts ♡, Diamonds ◇, and Clubs ♣.

When the cards are played, as will be described in more detail later, each player plays a card from his hand in clockwise rotation and it is an important rule that each player must follow suit. That is to say that if the first player plays a spade each of the others must also contribute a spade if they have one. If not they can follow with any card they like.

Tricks

As bridge is a game involving taking tricks it is necessary to explain at this stage what is meant by a trick. Take this simple example.

4 of spades

N

2 of spades W E King of spades

S

Ace of spades

Suppose that West leads the two of spades, North plays the four of spades, East the king of spades and South the ace of spades. These four cards (one from each player) constitute a trick and the highest card played (in this case the ace) will win. These four cards are gathered together into a small pack and placed in front of one or other of the partners face down.

It is a rule of the game that the player who wins a trick leads to the following trick. In the example, South, who won the trick with the ace of spades, would lead to the next trick. He may lead any card of any suit.

It does not matter which partner keeps the tricks, but it is a rule of the game that the tricks should be arranged neatly in order so that they can be identified.

The ace, being the highest card of the suit, will nearly always win a trick. But there is one situation where the ace could be beaten – if it is trumped.

Trumps

A trump is a card of a specified suit that, for the purpose of the particular deal, has precedence over all the other suits for trick taking purposes. The trump suit is established by the bidding, as will be described later.

The effect of a trump can be seen in the next example.

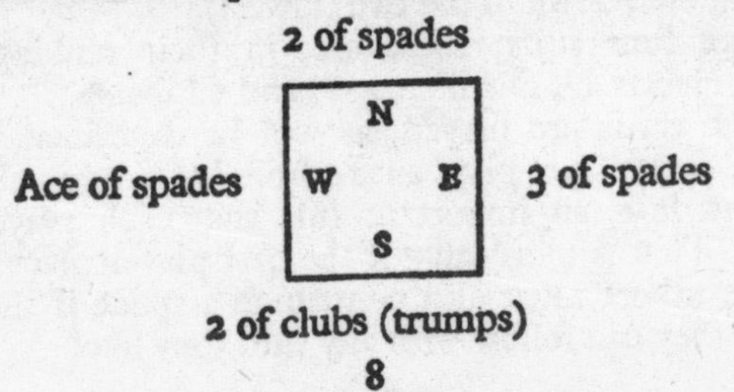

West leads the ace of spades which can fully be expected to take the trick. Both North and East follow suit but South has no spade. But he has a club, a card of the trump suit. Although his club is only the two, the lowest card in the pack, he will nevertheless win the trick as he has trumped the ace of spades. He might also be said to have ruffed the ace, as the term 'ruff' is the same as 'trump'.

Object of the Game

To understand the object of the game it is best to see an ordinary bridge scorer which looks like this –

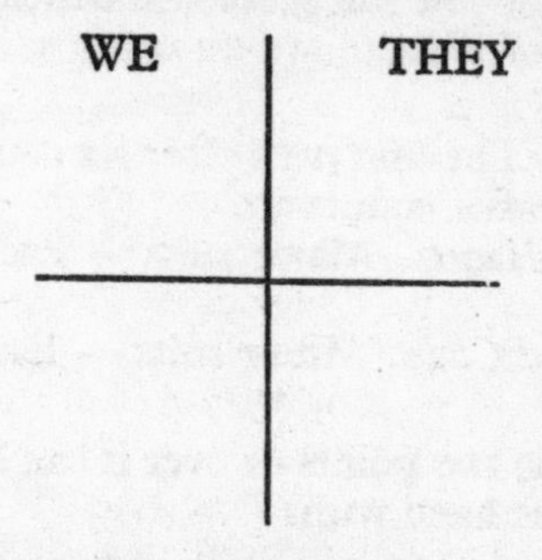

The line down the middle separates our score from that of our opponents. The horizontal line across the centre is important as it separates the scores that go towards making a game (see below) and those that are bonus scores.

The primary object is to win two games which means that you win one rubber. To make a game you need to score 100 points or more below the horizontal line.

When a rubber has been completed, one side having won two games, the scores are added up. Each side adds up all the points scored, both above and below the line. The side with the greater total wins and, if there is a monetary stake, per hundred points of winning margin, the score is computed correct to the nearest hundred. E.g. 850 difference would count as 8 (hundred) points, but 860 would count as 9.

To score below the line you must bid and make what is termed a contract. That is to say, you and your partner must undertake to win a given number of tricks over and above six, either with a suit as trumps or without any trump suit (No Trumps).

The reason that a contract involves taking a certain number of tricks above six is this. In every deal each player starts with thirteen cards. If he plays one card at a time there will be thirteen tricks. Mathematically, out of these, one side or the other must win at least seven. So the seventh trick is the odd trick and equal to a contract of one.

Thus to call a contract bid of:

1 *spade* means that you reckon to win at least seven tricks with spades as trumps.

3 *diamonds* means that you reckon to win at least nine tricks with diamonds as trumps.

The amount that you will score will depend on the suit that becomes trumps or if there are no trumps. The values are as follows:

No Trumps – The first trick after six counts 40 points and each trick thereafter counts 30.

Spades and Hearts (Major suits) – Each trick above six counts 30.

Diamonds and Clubs (Minor suits) – Each trick above six counts 20.

As a game needs 100 points or over it can be seen that game can be made in one hand with:

3 No Trumps (40+30+30) = 100
4 Spades or 4 Hearts (30+30+30+30) = 120
5 Diamonds or 5 Clubs (20+20+20+20+20) = 100

It is more difficult to make game in diamonds or clubs as they count so little. It is best to aim at playing in no trumps or spades or hearts.

It may not be possible to make enough tricks to score 100 points in one deal. If you settle for a lower contract and succeed you will have a 'part score'. That is to say you will have something towards your 100 and will only need to make up the balance next time.

Example. You play a contract of 2 spades and make (win) 8 tricks. You score 60 points below the line (2 × 30). Suppose you had made 10 tricks. You would then have scored 60 points below the line and 60 points above. Only the 60 points below the line will count towards game (100) as that was all you contracted to make. The 60 for the other two tricks will all be scored when you add up at the end, but they are bonus scores. Had you bid 4 spades, i.e. had you contracted to win four tricks over the six and succeeded, you would have scored 120 points below the line (game).

In explaining the difference between scoring above and below the line it has been necessary to refer to the bidding, which means the number of tricks that the partnership undertakes to win. This aspect of the game will become clearer when we describe the auction.

We said earlier that the primary object of the game is to win two games and score a rubber. This carries with it a bonus which goes above the line. The bonus is:

700 points if one side wins 2 games and their opponents score no game (2–0)

500 if one side wins 2 games and their opponents score one game (2–1)

Tennis players can compare this to a tennis match consisting of three sets. If one player wins the first two sets it is game, set and match (= 700 bonus points and rubber). If his opponent wins the second set and he wins the deciding set it is similar to a 500 bonus rubber win.

Space here does not allow a completely detailed description of all the scoring, but the scoring table on p. 122 contains the complete necessary information. Nevertheless it may be as well to make brief mention of what happens if a player fails to make the number of tricks that he contracted on behalf of his partnership to do. For example, South bids 3 hearts and instead of taking nine tricks (6 + 3) he ends up with only seven. He is two down (undertricks). He loses penalty points to his opponents, which they score above the line. The amount he loses depends on whether he is VULNERABLE or NOT VULNERABLE during the hand concerned.

A side becomes *vulnerable* when they have made one game. Having one leg of the rubber and being in a better position than their opponents they are handicapped in that the penalties when they fail are bigger. Certain bonuses are increased also, but it is usually wise to be a bit more careful when you are vulnerable and you are not too certain of success.

Another term that appears on the scoring table that needs explanation is DOUBLE. If your opponent makes a bid that you do not consider he will be able to fulfil you say 'double'. If he fails in his contract the penalty will be greater. If he succeeds, his score is doubled and he receives a small bonus above the line of 50 for the doubled contract.

Other items of scoring which need explanation are these –

Honours

These are the ace, king, queen, knave and ten. If a player holds all five honours in his own hand and the honours are in the trump suit he can claim a bonus of 150 points, scored above the line. If he holds any four he can claim 100. The bonus is scored irrespective of whether the player succeeds or fails in his contract, or whether he is declarer or defender (see below). Also if a player holds all four aces in his hand and the contract is being played in No Trumps, he can claim 150. It is normal practice to claim the honours bonus at the end of the hand.

Slams

A player who contracts to win all thirteen tricks, and succeeds, scores a Grand Slam. If he contracts to make all except one he scores a Little or Small Slam. As the scoring table shows, these carry quite a large bonus, larger when the contracting side has already won one game (i.e. is vulnerable).

General Procedure

When the four players sit down to play bridge it is usual to cut for partners. That is to say, the pack is spread out across the table face downwards and each player detaches a card at random and turns it upwards. The players with the two highest cards play as partners against those with the two lowest. If two players cut a card of equal rank, the ranking order of the suits applies. This is

Spades ♠
Hearts ♡ (Alphabetical order,
Diamonds ◇ upside down.)
Clubs ♣

The player who cuts the highest card is the dealer and he is entitled to two small privileges:

(1) He may select where he wishes to sit. Some players are superstitious and think that a particular seat is lucky.

(2) He can choose which coloured pack to use. One side deals with one coloured pack and the other side with the other.

Of course, if there is a pre-arrangement whereby two players have agreed to play together against two others, the cut is solely for deal and choice of seats, etc., but not to determine who plays together.

The player on the immediate left of the dealer shuffles the pack (often referred to as 'making' the cards) and passes them to the dealer who is entitled to a final shuffle. He passes them to the player on his right who cuts the pack by dividing it roughly into half. The dealer completes the cut by placing the two portions back together, the lower one now being upon the top of the pack, and proceeds to deal the cards clockwise, face downwards, one at a time, to each player. At the end of the deal each player will have thirteen cards. These he sorts out into suits in his hand, holding the cards in such a way as not to be visible to any other players. The deal passes clockwise round the table, so that if South, in the diagram below, deals the first hand, West will deal the next and so on. Dealer's partner meanwhile shuffles the other pack and places it on his right.

The Auction

The dealer is entitled to make the first bid. We shall examine the principles on which he should bid in Part 2. For the moment we shall say that in very broad terms if he holds a good hand he will bid and if he has a bad hand 'No bid'.

Once the bidding has started, it proceeds in a clockwise manner round the table, each bid being higher than the previous one. A player who bids in a higher ranking suit can do so at the same level or number of tricks; otherwise he must increase the bid.

No trumps ranks, for bidding purposes, higher than any of the suits. This is in accordance with their greater points value as set out on page 10. Therefore 1 no trump will be sufficient to outbid 1 spade, 1 heart, 1 diamond or 1 club.

The auction remains alive until three players pass, by saying 'No bid', in succession. At this point the auction comes to an end and the final bid becomes the final contract.

Here is an example, where South is the dealer:

South opens one spade and West bids two clubs. North supports South and bids two spades and then East bids three diamonds. South follows with 'No bid' as also does West. But North now bids three spades and all the other three players pass with 'No bid'. The auction has finished and the final contract is three spades. That is to say North and South have contracted to win at least nine tricks (6 + 3) with spades as trumps.

An auction at bridge is similar to that in a saleroom. If a piece of furniture is put up for sale and someone bids £10 and someone increases to £12, and then eventually after a bid of £20 the auctioneer says 'Going, going, gone, knocked down to Mr. South for £20', Mr. South has bought the item. In the example above, when three players said 'No bid' after North's bid of three spades, the contract was *bought* by North–South.

The trump suit has been established as a result of the bidding, as also has the number of tricks to be taken.

The first player to name the suit or denomination that becomes the final contract is called the *declarer*. Here South is declarer because he first called one spade, and the players on his left and right are the *defenders*.

Playing a hand

The defender on the left of the declarer makes the opening lead by placing a card face upwards on the table. Immediately after this the declarer's partner (North) lays all his cards face upwards on the table, sorted into suits with the trumps (if any) on his right. North is called *Dummy* and he has no active part in the play of that hand. He cannot make any suggestions or offer to help. He has some rights which you need not worry about at this stage.

South, the declarer, plays both hands (his own and dummy's) and tries to make the number of tricks he has contracted to win. The defenders' aim is to prevent this happening. In our example, where the final contract is three spades, South must try and win nine tricks and if he succeeds he will score 90 points below the line (nearly game). The defenders in this instance must try and take at least five tricks to prevent the declarer making his contract of three. If they are successful they will score points by way of penalty and these will be scored above the line.

To end Part 1 we will illustrate the play of two hands.

In the first hand we will assume that the bidding has ended with South as declarer in a final contract of *four hearts*, which means that South must win ten tricks in all (6 + 4) to succeed.

West leads the ace of spades, after which North places his thirteen cards on the table with the trumps (hearts in this instance) on his right. In order to follow the play we will expose all the four hands:

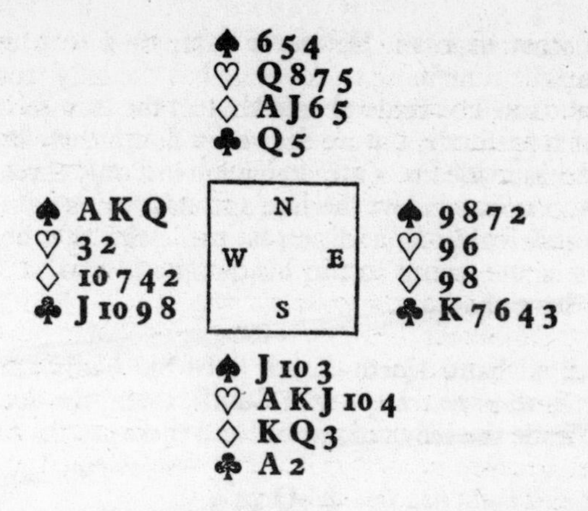

West wins the first trick, the four, two and three of spades being played by each of the other players. West continues with the king of spades and, again, the other three players follow suit by playing a spade. West, having won the second trick, plays the queen of spades and once again all players are able to follow with a spade. West now leads the knave of clubs and South tries to win the trick with dummy's queen, but East plays the king and South has to win the trick with his ace.

It is now South's lead and he plays hearts (trumps). He wants to draw the trumps from his opponents' hands and after two rounds which he wins by playing the ace and next the king, he has attained his object. When each opponent has given a card to the two rounds of trumps they will have played four in all. As South and dummy had 9 between them, all the trumps will have been drawn from the opponents. His chief worry is that he may lose a trick in clubs as he has a low card in each hand (his own and dummy's). But he is able to avoid this by playing diamonds. He first leads the king which takes the trick and next the queen which also wins. Both opponents, of course, play diamonds to these tricks as they have to follow suit. Next South plays the three of diamonds and the trick is won by dummy's knave. East has no diamond to play and cannot follow suit. If he had a trump he could use it but South was careful to draw the trumps first. So East discards a club. As dummy won the previous trick with the knave of diamonds, the lead is in the North hand (dummy) and the ace of diamonds enables South to throw away, or discard, his two of clubs. South cannot follow suit having run out of diamonds and can discard what he likes. He is *not* compelled to trump. South must win the remaining tricks as he has the only trumps left in his hand. It will be remembered that all the trumps held by the opponents (defenders) were drawn by South early in the game.

South has made his contract, having lost only three tricks. He scores 120 points below the line and has won a game. *His side becomes vulnerable.* In addition he can claim that he held four honours in the trump suit in his own hand and will score 100 points above the line.

On the next hand North–South have bid badly and the final contract is *three no trumps* with South, again, the declarer.

West leads the ace of diamonds and these are the four hands:

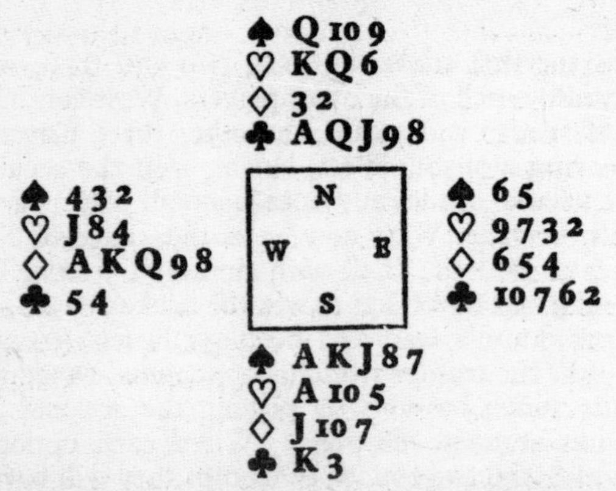

West wins the first trick with the ace of diamonds and continues with the king and next with the queen. The dummy hand cannot follow suit in the third round and as there are no trumps can only throw away a card from some other suit, such as a club. After three tricks all won by West with his top diamonds, no other player has a diamond in his hand. With no trumps, this means that there is no way of preventing West from winning two more tricks by leading his remaining two diamonds and thus taking a total of five tricks and defeating the contract. After losing the first five tricks it can be calculated that South will make the rest as, between himself and his dummy, he has all the top cards.

Bad bidding cost the game, because had North and South made spades the trumps West would not have been able to win so many tricks. He would have been stopped after two rounds by a trump card from the dummy, who only held two diamonds to begin with.

At the end of these two hands North–South's score card would look like this:

WE	THEY
100	100
120	

The 100 points on the right would be the penalty for going one trick down vulnerable (one *undertrick*).

Part One Quiz

1. Mr. & Mrs. Smith and Mr. & Mrs. Jones sit down to play bridge and agree to cut for partners. They cut as follows:
   Mr. Smith draws the king of spades
   Mrs. Smith draws the ten of diamonds
   Mr. Jones draws the ten of hearts
   Mrs. Jones draws the six of spades.
   (a) Which two play as partners against the others?
   (b) Who is dealer?
2. After the deal, how many cards should each player hold?
3. South opens the bidding with one heart and North, his partner, bids three hearts. There is no further bidding.
   (a) Who is declarer and plays the hand?
   (b) Who makes the opening lead?
   (c) How many tricks does the declarer need to make?
   (d) Which suit is trumps?
4. The final contract is two spades played by North as declarer. He makes eleven tricks.
   (a) How is this scored?
   (b) Has he made a game?
5. When does a side become vulnerable?
6. South plays a contract of three no trumps and makes nine tricks. He held all five honours in clubs in his hand.
   (a) What does he score?
   (b) Does he score game?
7. How many tricks can you afford to lose if you bid
   (a) Grand Slam?
   (b) Little Slam?
8. If you fail to make your contract can you still claim a bonus for honours?

Answers to Part One Quiz

1. (a) Mr. Jones and Mr. Smith play together against the two wives. Mr. Jones, having drawn the ten of hearts, is partner to Mr. Smith (king of spades) as hearts is a higher ranking suit than diamonds.
   (b) Mr. Smith who drew the highest card.
2. Thirteen
3. (a) South, who first mentioned hearts
   (b) West, on the left of South
   (c) Nine (6 + 3)
   (d) Hearts
4. (a) 60 points below the line (only two spades bid) and 90 points above the line (3 × 30 for overtricks).
   (b) No
5. When they have scored one game towards a rubber.
6. (a) 100 points below the line. No score for honours as clubs were not trumps.
   (b) Yes.
7. (a) None
   (b) One
8. Yes.

PART TWO

THE BIDDING

In discussing the bidding it will be convenient to abbreviate bids by first putting the number and then the symbol of the suit or NT for no trump. e.g. 1 ♠ = one spade, 2 ♣ = two clubs, 1 NT = one no trump.

In Part 1 it was explained that it is only possible to score below the line and win games by bidding what you thought you would make.

In order to make the best of your cards it is essential for two partners to have some common understanding whereby they can describe to each other the nature and quality of the hand they possess and thereby assess how many tricks they consider they can win jointly and which suit, if any, it would be wise to have as trumps. For this purpose it is necessary to have a mutually understood system for the Bidding. There are numerous systems, some more simple than others. The two systems most popular in England, both fairly straightforward and natural, are:

(1) *The 2 Clubs System.* This derives its name from one special bid of 2 ♣ which signifies a very strong hand (see page 38).

(2) *Acol.* This is in many ways similar to the 2 Clubs system. The system derived its name because, before World War II, a group of leading players used to play in a club in Hampstead, London, called the Acol Bridge Club as it was situated in Acol Road, N.W.6. In the necessarily fairly short coverage of bidding in this book the methods recommended will be applicable to both systems mentioned above. Should there be any important differences they will be stated.

Valuation

Purely as a guide as to the strength of your hand for bidding purposes all systems employ a simple method of counting points for the honour cards, as follows:

For each ace you hold count, 4 points.
For each king you hold count, 3 points.
For each queen you hold count, 2 points.
For each knave you hold count, 1 point.

The ten is sometimes valued at half a point; if you do not wish to get tangled up with fractions it is perfectly satisfactory if you regard it as an asset. When the top cards have been played the lower cards such as tens and even nines come into their own, and to hold, say, K 10 8 looks better than K 4 2, though each contains only 3 points (the king).

A simple count will show that each suit contains 10 points (A + K + Q + J) and as there are four suits the total pack contains 40 points.

If you and your partner were able to discover that you held between you all 40 points it would be easy to call a Grand Slam, contracting to make all 13 tricks, as you would have all the high cards.

Needless to say this hardly ever happens, but it is possible to discover that your side possesses the larger share.

An average hand contains 10 points (a quarter of 40). As an opening bid literally implies that the bidder is prepared to take at least 7 tricks it is reasonable to assume that his hand should be above the average. It is asking too much that he should have seven probable tricks in his own hand. He is entitled to hope that his partner will be able to contribute something.

So, as a start, we will recommend that any hand containing 13 points or more will always qualify for an opening bid as it represents the value of one king (3 points) above average.

Opening Bids of One in a Suit

Before discussing hands of 13 or more points that automatically qualify as an opening bid, it may be as well to consider hands just below that value (13). It is wrong to assume that you must pass if you do not hold 13 points. But you must hold compensating strength by way of distribution.

Consider these two hands:

	A.		B.
	♠ A K 7 6		♠ A K 9 7 6
A.	♡ A 4 3	B.	♡ A 4 3
	◇ J 7 6		◇ J 7 6
	♣ 8 4 3		♣ 8 4
	12 points		12 points

Hand A is unlikely to win more than three tricks by itself. The ace and king of spades should win and also the ace of hearts, but after that it is doubtful if you would make any more.

Hand B is better as you hold 5 spades. This means that the other three players have 8 between them. Assume, then, that these are divided as equally as possible, e.g.

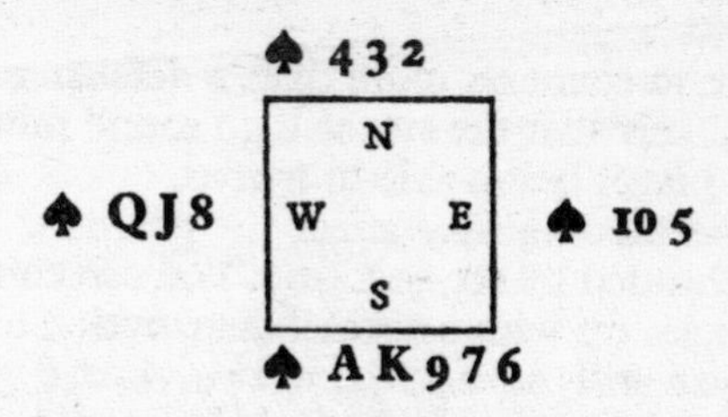

When the ace of spades is led, West follows suit with the eight, North with the two and East with the five. On the king of spades West plays the knave, North plays the three and East the ten. On the third round West wins with the queen; North plays the four; East has no more and throws a card of another suit. This leaves South with the only two remaining spades which will take tricks provided no-one can follow suit and they cannot trump.

A long suit is therefore an advantage. Some players like to count an extra value for a short suit in their hand. This is wrong; it may be an embarrassment to have to trump because you may run short of trumps. A short suit should only be considered of value in the supporting hand as we will explain later.

In every hand a certain number of tricks are won with high cards such as aces and kings and a certain number with small cards which become established in the manner described above, where the five card spade suit was likely to produce extra tricks by virtue of its length.

Therefore, if you hold a long suit you can afford to dispense with *some* high cards. But if you hold an evenly balanced hand, where the longest suit contains only four cards, you are not likely to win many tricks with low cards and you are largely dependent on the aces and kings.

Hence the need for 13 or more points when there is no long suit.

A simple yardstick to cover hands with less than 13 points is –

Open with 12 points if you hold a reasonable 5 card suit

Open with 10–11 points if you hold a reasonable 6 card suit or two 5 card suits.

In addition the hand should be worth two defensive tricks. That is to say, the hand should be likely to take at least 2 tricks, even if the opposing side play the contract and you defend.

It is not safe to count on more than 2 defensive tricks in one suit as it is unlikely that the suit will go round more than twice without some player being able to trump.

Similarly the bidding may affect the position. Suppose you hold 6 spades headed by ace and king. You can count on having 2 defensive tricks, for with a normal distribution of the remainder each player will have at least two. But if your partner supported you to four spades, which he would only do if he held at least four cards in the suit, you would have ten out of thirteen spades between you and it would not be surprising if the opponents were able to trump the first round should the final contract fall to a different suit.

Before leaving the question of opening bids with hands below 13 points it should be emphasized that the player who makes the opening bid enjoys many tactical advantages, including putting the opponents, at least temporarily, on the defensive. It should also be said that it is much safer to open with a bid at the one level than to wait and come in later at the level of two or more.

Examples of OPENING Bids on hands with *less* than 13 points

(a) ♠ A K 10 8 6
♡ K 10 7 6
◇ Q 5 4
♣ 4
Bid 1 ♠

(b) ♠ A 2
♡ K Q J 9 8 6
◇ 10 8 6
♣ 7 6
Bid 1 ♡

(c) ♠ A Q J 7 5
♡ K J 7 6 3
◇ 8 5
♣ 3
Bid 1 ♠

(d) ♠ K Q 6 3 2
♡ K 7 4
◇ Q 7 6
♣ Q 3
Pass. Despite 12 points the suit has no substance

Opening Bids with 13 or more Points

A hand containing at least 13 points in high cards is, in value, a king above the average, as explained already. The problem is not whether to open or pass. It is *what* to bid.

Firstly, a suit to be biddable, must consist of at least four cards. This is a fundamental principle based upon commonsense.

When you bid a suit it is at least a tentative suggestion that it will be trumps. (If you hold only three cards in a suit, then mathematically one player at the table must hold four. As there are two opponents and one partner, it is 2–1 against your partner holding four. But the purpose of selecting a trump suit is to control the hand and you must have a majority of the trumps.)

Secondly, the suit should have some substance. As a major suit is more likely to be supported immediately it needs to be stronger, containing at least two honours, one of which is queen or better, for example:

(a) **A J 4 3** (b) **Q 10 6 5** (c) **K J 7 6**

A minor suit is less likely to become the final trump suit and can be bid on less, e.g. 10 4 3 2: J 7 6 2

If you have more than one biddable suit it is important to call the right suit first. The choice is governed by an important principle that is common to virtually all systems: That is that it is an understood thing that when a player opens the bidding he promises to give his partner a second opportunity to bid if he responds initially by calling a different suit at the minimum level. The only exception to this is where the partner has already said 'No Bid', thereby denying the values for an opening bid.

The reason for this principle is simple. Your partner may hold a good hand, containing say 13–14 points which should be enough to justify a game contract. But it may not be possible for him to show the full strength of his hand on the first round owing to lack of information. On the next round he should know enough and he must therefore be given the opportunity.

In technical language a change of suit by responder is 'forcing for one round'. This means that if the opener's partner (responder) bids a different suit the opener is forced to bid once more, as he would be in these two examples:

(a)	S	N	(b)	S	N
	1 ♢	1 ♠		1 ♡	2 ♢

Consider these two hands:

West		East
♠ K Q 9 6	N	♠ J 5 4
♡ A Q 7 5	W E	♡ 6 4
♢ 4 3		♢ A K 10 7 6
♣ Q 5 4	S	♣ 8 7 6

Suppose we assume the opponents remain silent. West opens 1 ♠ and East replies 2 ♢ West next calls 2 ♡ to show the second suit. East has a modest hand and merely wishes to convey that he would rather have spades as trumps. He does this by bidding 2 ♠. Suppose you interchange his spades and hearts, giving him ♠ 6 4 and ♡ J 5 4. Now he will pass after the 2 ♡ implying that the second suit is better for him.

Consider what would have happened if West had opened 1 ♡ and re-bid 2 ♠ over 2 ♢. East would not have liked to leave his partner in 2 ♠ with two low cards, but 3 ♡ would have been too high. The difficulty arose because West opened the wrong suit.

In order to follow the principle explained above some rules of thumb should help:

With two four card suits open with the higher ranking suit first. This holds good only if the suits are adjacent in ranking order. With four spades and four clubs for example, you would open 1 ♣.

A simple rule which covers all hands divided 4-4-3-2 is: open with the suit ranking immediately below the doubleton (suit with 2 cards). If that is not biddable go on down the order to the next, e.g.

(a) ♠ A J 7 2
♡ 4 3
♢ A K 10 6
♣ Q 7 5
Open 1 ♢

(b) ♠ A J 7 2
♡ 4 3
♢ Q 5 2
♣ A Q 8 6
Open 1 ♣. Suit below doubleton is diamonds; not biddable so pass on to clubs.

We explained earlier (page 23) the need for the opener to make a further bid if his partner responded in a new suit. The question of rebids will be described in a later chapter (page 45).

In Example (a) above the opener will rebid 1 ♠ if partner responds 1 ♡. If partner responds to 1 ◇ with 2 ♣ the opener will support to 3 ♣.

In example (b) opener will rebid 1 ♠ if partner responds either 1 ◇ or 1 ♡ to the opening bid of 1 ♣.

With two five card suits, open with the higher ranking one, except with five clubs and 5 spades. In this case open 1 ♣ and re-bid 1 ♠, e.g.

(c) ♠ A J 9 6 4
♡ Q 3
◇ K Q 10 8 6
♣ 8
Open 1 ♠

(d) ♠ A Q 10 7 5
♡ 4 3
◇ 6
♣ A K 9 8 6
Open 1 ♣; re-bid 1 ♠.

In an instance like (d) above if partner bids again, you then repeat spades. Such a re-bid (repeat) of a suit by a player, which has not been supported, promises at least five cards in the suit.

If the opening-biddable suits are different in length, open with the longer one.

Sometimes a re-bid by the opener in the second of two biddable suits forces his partner to show a preference for the first suit at the three level; the opener should avoid this unless he holds a strong hand of about 16 points e.g. (a hand with 16 points)

♠ A Q 9 7
♡ K Q 10 8 6
◇ A J 2
♣ 3

Open with 1 ♡. If partner responds 2 ♣ or 2 ◇ bid 2 ♠ next. This virtually compels your partner to bid 3 ♡ in order to put you back to your first suit if he prefers it. But you have a good hand and your hearts are longer than your spades.

Most opening bids are made at the level of one as it is desirable that your partner should be allowed to indicate what he holds at a low level. Thus for an opening bid of one in a suit your points may range between 10–11 including a six card suit, up to a possible 19. With more than 19 points an alternative opening bid is likely to be made.

Opening Bid Quiz

What do you open on –

(a) ♠ A K Q
♡ 8 7 6 4 3
◇ J 7 6
♣ J 3

(b) ♠ K Q J 9 8 6
♡ A J 6
◇ 4 3
♣ 7 6

(c) ♠ 7 6
♡ 10 8
◇ A K Q 10 8 6
♣ J 5 2

(d) ♠ K Q 8 6
♡ A K J 2
◇ J 4 3
♣ 6 5

(e) ♠ K J 4 3
♡ K 2
◇ Q 7 5
♣ A Q 10 6

(f) ♠ J 5
♡ Q J 10 6 2
◇ A Q J 8
♣ K 3

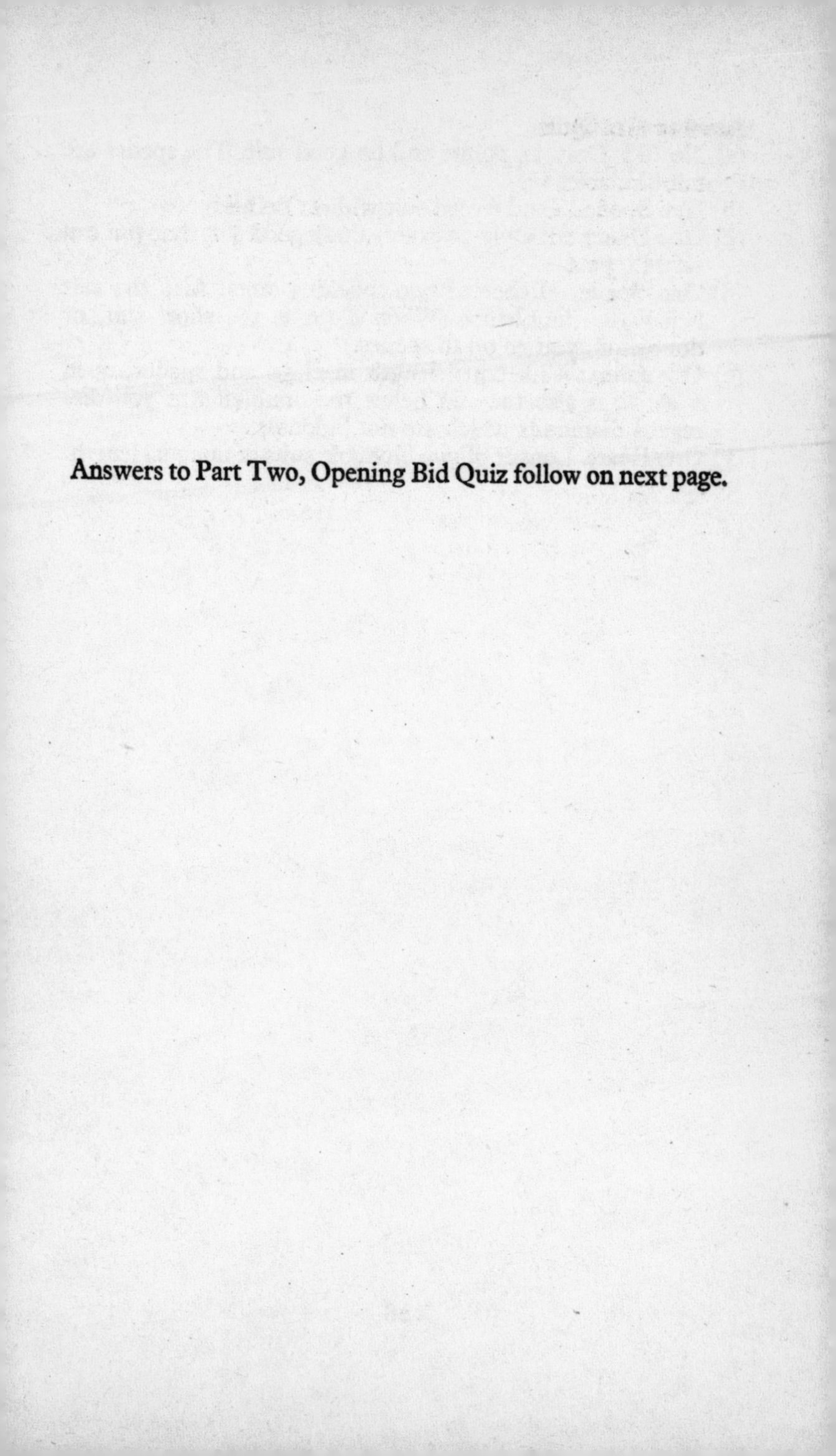

Answers to Part Two, Opening Bid Quiz follow on next page.

Answers to Quiz

(a) No Bid. Only 11 points and no good suit. The spades are not biddable.

(b) One Spade. Good 6 card suit with 11 points.

(c) One Diamond. Only 10 points but a good suit that you can safely repeat.

(d) One Spade. Higher of two touching suits. Also the suit below the doubleton. (When clubs is the short suit, or doubleton, you go on to spades.)

(e) One Club. With equal length in clubs and spades, open 1 ♣. It is also the suit below the doubleton as you disregard diamonds which are not biddable.

(f) One Heart. Longer of two biddable suits of unequal length.

RESPONSE TO OPENING SUIT BIDS

As the opening bid may cover a large range it is important to ensure that the opener has a further chance. Suppose the dealer bids 1 ♡ and the other three players pass; the auction would be ended.

To avoid this the minimum strength you need look for to keep the bidding open, in considering the responding hand, is 6 points.

It follows that with a very weak (minimum) hand it is desirable to find the cheapest bid. Here is an example:

Assume partner opens 1 ♠ and the next player says No Bid; and you hold,

♠ 9 4 3
♡ J 7 5
◇ K 10 8 4
♣ Q 9 7

A total of 6 points and enough to respond. Diamonds is your longest suit, but to bid 2 ◇ would increase the number of tricks to make from 7 to 8. You cannot reasonably support spades and the only bid that does not increase the contract is 1 NT.

This implies –

(1) A weak hand of 6–9 points
(2) Not much support for partner's suit
(3) That it is the most economical bid.

Given an improved hand such as this,

♠ 9 4 3
♡ Q 10 8
◇ K 10 7 5
♣ A Q 4

You have 11 points plus two tens and an even hand. Evenly divided hands are usually associated with no trumps. As you are too good to bid 1 NT, you bid 2 NT. Had you been a little stronger you could have bid 3 NT.

Normally a response of:

1 NT = 6–9 points, 2 NT = 11–12, 3 NT = 13–15.

Hands containing 10 points are awkward. If they contain good intermediate cards such as tens and nines they may justify stretching the response to 2 NT. More often it is better to make a simple response in a new suit.

Consider this hand and assume the opening bid is 1 ♡.

You hold,

♠ 4 3
♡ Q 10 7 5
◇ K 10 6 4
♣ Q 4 2

You can help your partner in hearts. He has at least four so that you hold at least eight between you. The fact that you hold only two spades is an asset as, once they are played you will be able to trump spades with your *supporting* trumps. So you raise 1 ♡ to 2 ♡. The single raise promises trump support, which should comprise four if possible. Occasionally you may support with only three, including an honour, but this may mean that you have only seven trumps against the other side's six. The overall strength of the hand will be about 6–9 points as with 1 NT, the difference being that you have support for the opener's suit.

Again given hands such as these:

(a)		(b)	
	♠ 4 2		♠ 4 2
	♡ Q 10 8 6		♡ Q 10 7 5
	◇ K 9 6 2		◇ A J 10 6 2
	♣ A Q 5		♣ K 4

In each case respond 3 ♡, which *guarantees* at least four of partner's suit and about 10–11 points or a little less with good distribution.

On hand (b) there is no need to show the diamonds. Try for game in the major suit which needs only ten tricks (4 × 30 = 120). Bidding 3 ♡ also makes it more difficult for the opponents to compete against you, possibly in spades.

A 1 ♡ – 4 ♡ raise to game would suggest a distributional hand, such as

♠ 2
♡ Q 10 7 6 4
◇ A Q 9 7 4
♣ 7 6

This is a good hand *if hearts are trumps.* It will not be much use in defence. You bid 4 ♡ to make it difficult for the opponents to enter the bidding cheaply. When you hold a lot of cards in your partner's suit try to buy the contract as quickly as you can.

The responses in no trumps and raising partner's suit are referred to as *limit bids.* This term means that your bid has described the full value of your hand within a narrow range. Your partner is therefore able to judge whether it is worth going on. If he sees no future, he can pass. In other words, a limit bid is not forcing. It does not compel your partner to bid again and this is because he can judge the combined strength quite accurately.

It is not always possible for the responder to show his full values on the first round. He may need more information and he obtains this by bidding a different suit.

Assume the opening bid is 1 ♣ and you hold,

♠ K 9 4 3
♡ K 8 5 2
◇ 10 4 2
♣ 6 5

A total of 6 points and therefore enough to respond. The cheapest bid for you is 1 ♡ and this will enable another bid to be found at a low level e.g. if your partners hand is,

(a)		(b)	
	♠ A J 6 5		♠ J 6
	♡ J 3		♡ A J 6 5
	◇ 7 6 5		◇ 7 6
	♣ A Q J 8		♣ A Q J 8 4

he will rebid 1 ♠ and you can support to 2 ♠. Alter the hand to (b) and he can then support 1 ♡ to 2 ♡. With a choice of four card suits to respond, bid the cheapest.

Your hand may not be so weak. Consider these:

(a)		(b)	
	♠ K Q 3		♠ K 6 4
	♡ A K 8 7 3		♡ 6 3
	◇ Q 10 4		◇ K Q 10 8
	♣ 4 2		♣ A Q 8 3

You hold hand (a) and partner's opening bid is 1 ♣. You hold 14 points, equal to an opening bid. As partner has opened you can hope for game. But you cannot bid game straight away as you do not know enough about his hand. Therefore respond

1 ♡. If he supports you to 2 ♡, bid 4 ♡. If he re-bids 2 ♣ or 1 NT suggesting lack of support for your suit, bid 3 NT.

With hand (b) your partner has opened 1 ♠ and you hold 14 points, but again you are unable to fix the contract at this stage. Bid 2 ♣, a change of suit that guarantees a further bid from your partner. At the two level this promises at least 8–9 points. Suppose he bids 2 ♠. By repeating the suit he can be assumed to hold at least five. You hold three, making a total of eight, so you can raise him in spades. The only problem is how far. Ask yourself whether you could have opened the bidding if it had been your turn. As the answer is 'Yes', you bid game – 4 ♠.

Suppose that instead of repeating the spades he bids 2 ♡. Now you bid 3 NT. The only reason that you did not bid 3 NT earlier was the fact that you might both be weak in the same suit. Now that he has bid hearts you are not worried.

The simple way to look at it is this. If you are in doubt as to the best final contract and you would like more information, bid a new suit and hear what your partner says next.

Sometimes you are fortunate enough to hold a very strong hand opposite the opening bid, with 16 points or more. You are not worried about not making game but you have ambitious thoughts about making a slam, that is taking all the tricks (grand slam), or all except one (small slam) and getting a large bonus.

The first step is to make a jump bid in a new suit at a level *exactly one higher* than was necessary to outbid the last call, e.g. 1 ♠–3 ♣ or 1 ♡–2 ♠. As it is legally necessary to bid 2 ♣ in order to outbid 1 ♠ (clubs being a lower ranking suit) a response of 3 ♣ represents a hand that is exactly one level higher than necessary. Similarly 1 ♡–2 ♠ is a jump bid at a level one higher than necessary, since 1 ♠ would be legally sufficient to outbid 1 ♡. A response of 2 NT to an opening bid of one in a suit (e.g. 1 ♡ or 1 ◇) is *NOT a jump bid* in a new suit and NOT FORCING. In fact 2 NT is a limit bid indicating 11–12 points (very occasionally 10, as discussed on page 30). This jump bid in a new suit ensures that the bidding is not allowed to stop before a contract has been reached which will be sufficient to make a game (e.g. 4 ♠: 3 NT: 5 ♣). In other words neither partner should pass a bid that is insufficient to make game. This allows the bidding to develop gradually so that each partner can obtain as much information as possible. It is generally referred to as 'forcing to game'.

If the opponents intervene the position is slightly altered insofar that the opener will be given a further chance to bid. Thus, suppose South opens 1 ♡ and West bids 1 ♠ and North holds:

♠ K 4 2
♡ 8 6 3
◇ Q 10 7 5
♣ J 8 6

He would have bid 1 NT had West passed, to give his partner another chance. But as West has bid, the auction will not end until South has had another turn, and therefore North can pass with his poor hand. A bid of 1 NT at this stage would suggest about 8–10 points with a stopper (high card) in spades, the opponent's suit. (Slightly more than the minimum 6–7 that he might hold to bid 1 NT after a pass by the second player.) The situation is slightly altered if North is in a position to support his partner's suit. In this case he should still raise, e.g. South opens 1 ♡ and West overcalls with 1 ♠. If North, with heart support, passes, East may raise spades and South is stuck, being unable to carry on single-handed. The initiative has been lost. But if North bids 2 ♡ South can compete if East supports his partners spades as he can at least count on support for his suit (hearts).

Responding Bid Quiz

1. Your partner, North, opens with 1 ♠, East passes. What do you say on

(a) ♠ Q 9 4 3
♡ 6 3
◇ K 7 6 4
♣ J 10 5

(b) ♠ 8 7 2
♡ Q 10 6
◇ K 10 6 2
♣ Q 8 3

(c) ♠ Q 2
♡ A J 4
◇ K J 7 6
♣ J 9 7 5

(d) ♠ Q 6 2
♡ A 10 5 3
◇ A 2
♣ K 10 8 6

(e) ♠ K J 9 7 5
♡ 3
◇ A Q 10 4 2
♣ 3 2

(f) ♠ 6 4 2
♡ Q 7 3
◇ Q 4 2
♣ J 4 3 2

2. Your partner, North, opens 1 ♣, East passes. What do you say on

(a) ♠ Q 8 4 2
♡ K 10 7 6
◇ Q 5 2
♣ 6 4

(b) ♠ A Q J 4 3
♡ A 4 2
◇ Q 8 3
♣ 6 5

(c) ♠ A 7 6
♡ K J 9
◇ K 10 8
♣ Q 10 6 5

(d) ♠ A 4 3
♡ A K J 9 6
◇ K Q 2
♣ Q 6

(e) ♠ A J 10 6 3
♡ 10 8
◇ K Q 6 2
♣ 7 5

(f) ♠ J 2
♡ Q 4 2
◇ J 4 3
♣ Q 10 7 5 2

Answers to Part Two Responding Bid Quiz follow on the next page.

Answers to Responder Quiz

1. (a) 2 ♠. Single raise promising 4 trumps. Implying 6–9 points.
   (b) 1 NT. 6–9 points. Not much support for spades. Cheapest bid.
   (c) 2 NT. 11–12 points evenly divided.
   (d) 2 ♣. This hand might be played in either spades, hearts or no trumps. Bid 2 ♣ and find out more about partner's hand.
   (e) 4 ♠. Based on distribution.
   (f) No Bid. Too few points.
2. (a) 1 ♡. Cheapest available bid.
   (b) 1 ♠. You hold the values for an opening bid, but you need to know more.
   (c) 3 NT. Balanced hand of 13 points and 2 tens. The most likely game contract.
   (d) 2 ♡. Forcing to game. Slam likely.
   (e) 1 ♠. If you get support game is possible.
   (f) 2 ♣. Not a good hand but club support.

OPENING BIDS IN NO TRUMPS

The opening bid of 1 NT shows an evenly divided hand. The shape will be 4–3–3–3 or, 4–4–3–2 or, 5–3–3–2. In other words the opener will have at least two cards in his shortest suit. He must not have only one (singleton) or none (void). He may hold a 5 card suit, but this must be a minor (diamonds or clubs) and not a major (spades or hearts). The reason for this is that games are rarely made in a minor suit requiring eleven tricks in all, when nine tricks in no trumps will be easier. A major suit only needs ten tricks for game.

The strength of the hand will depend upon partnership agreement as there are two distinct ranges, referred to as the Strong No Trump and the Weak No Trump. Before you start to play you must agree with your partner and tell him which range you are going to use should you make an opening bid of one no trump. Some players consider the opening strong no trump is better than the weak and vice versa; there are advantages both ways. You are also entitled to know what your opponents are doing.

Strong No Trump
An opening bid of one NT shows a balanced hand with 16–18 points. Alternative range 15–17.

e.g.	(a)		(b)	
		♠ K 8 6		♠ K 8 6
		♡ A J 4		♡ A Q
		◇ K 7 9 5		◇ K J 10 7 5
		♣ A J 5		♣ A 6 3
		16 points.		17 points. 5 card minor.

The responder is in a good position as he knows the type of hand his partner holds and also its strength within 2 points. He is not obliged to reply but will do so if he considers that he can improve on the contract either by raising it in the hope of making game or taking out into a suit if he considers it safer.

It is generally accepted that a combined total of 25–26 high card points will be sufficient to take nine tricks (game) in no trumps. If one player holds a long suit, you may succeed with less. So in raising no trumps you only do so if there is a possibility that the combined hands can total 25. If they cannot, pass unless you consider it to be safer to play with a suit as trumps.

In considering whether to raise no trumps always assume partner holds a minimum but allow for the possibility he has the maximum. Thus if you hold 0–7 points and no long suit, say – No Bid.

On balance it does not pay to raise with 7 points without a long suit. With 8 points – Raise to 2 NT.

Here you hold 24 points for certain. It may be 25–26, depending on partner's hand. If he has 17–18 he can then bid 3 NT. With a bare 16 he will pass.

With 9 points or over in your hand – Bid 3 NT as the partnership has at least 25 points.

examples:

(a)	(b)	(c)
♠ K 4 3	♠ K 6 4	♠ K 8 6
♡ Q 7 3	♡ Q 7 6 2	♡ Q 9 7
◇ J 6 4 2	◇ J 7 5	◇ K 7 5 4
♣ 8 7 6	♣ Q 8 4	♣ Q 7 3
No Bid.	Bid 2 NT.	Bid 3 NT.

A response to a no trumps bid in 2 of a suit, apart from clubs, is called a Weak Take-Out. It is made on a very weak hand, totally unsuited for no trumps, and your only reason for making the bid is that you consider that 2 in your suit is an improvement on 1 NT. The opener must pass.

If you hold a hand with game values (9 points or more) but unbalanced, force by bidding three of your suit. This is more usual with a major suit. With a minor suit raise no trumps. e.g.:

(d)	(e)
♠ A J 9 7 6	♠ 7 6 2
♡ K 8 4	♡ Q 4 2
◇ 3	◇ A K Q 8 4 2
♣ Q 10 6 3	♣ 7
Bid 3 ♠	Bid 3 NT.

Conventional Response of Two Clubs (STAYMAN Convention)

A response of 2 ♣ by the partner of the opener is conventional. That is to say it does not carry the meaning it appears to have. Conventional bids are usually artificial and they will only be understood by your partner if you have previously agreed on the bid. Private arrangements between two partners are, of course, forbidden. Certain conventional bids are, however, accepted. But they must be announced at the start of each rubber as the opponents are fully entitled to know what they mean. This conventional response of 2 ♣ was originally part of the Acol system. It was later developed by an American, Sam Stayman, and it has become known as the Stayman Convention.

Coming back to the response of 2 ♣, consider these two hands –

West		East
♠ K J 8 2	N	♠ Q 10 7 6
♡ A J 6	W E	♡ K Q 9 8
◇ A Q 3		◇ K J 4
♣ Q 10 2	S	♣ 5 4

Suppose West opens 1 NT: East could reply 3 NT. He has 11 points and is fairly balanced. But if clubs are led the defenders could easily win six tricks. You would have been safer in spades but, how can a spade contract be reached after an opening bid of 1 NT? East cannot bid 2 ♠ as that would be weakness and 3 ♠ would suggest a longer suit.

The solution is this conventional bid of 2 ♣. This asks the opener whether he holds four cards in a major suit. In this case he now bids 2 ♠ and East raises to 4 ♠. Had West held four hearts he would have responded 2 ♡, and East would bid 4 ♡.

West of course might not have held four cards of either major suit. In that case he bids 2 ◇ – again an artificial and conventional bid – stating he has not got four cards in either spades or hearts. This is quite logical as 2 ◇ is the cheapest bid over 2 ♣. Now East will naturally give up any ideas of playing in a major suit as there cannot be more than 7 cards at most in either. So he will revert to no trumps and bid 3 NT, having investigated the alternatives.

To employ this convention the responder should observe two qualifications:

(1) He must be interested in the possibility of playing the contract in a major suit as an alternative to no trumps. This means that he must have at least one, if not both, four card majors.

(2) He must be able to ensure the safety of the contract. This

means he should have at least 8 points as he may have to return to no trumps, and 1 NT–2 NT = 8 points. He may relax this condition if he holds one 5 card and one 4 card major as he can always retreat to the 5 card suit as a weak take-out.

If the responder holds a long string of clubs and a weak hand he bids 2 ♣ and follows up with 3 ♣ as sign off.

Examples: Opener 1 NT. (15–17.)

(a) ♠ AJ76
♡ 42
◇ KQ86
♣ J86

Bid 2 ♣. Raise 2 ♠ to 4 ♠. Bid 3 NT over 2 ◇ or 2 ♡.

(b) ♠ Q643
♡ K1075
◇ J43
♣ 86

No Bid. You cannot afford to bid 2 NT if opener bids 2 ◇ (should he have no 4 card major).

(c) ♠ Q864
♡ J9862
◇ 1053
♣ 6

Bid 2 ♣. Pass 2 ♡ or 2 ♠. Bid 2 ♡ over 2 ◇.

(d) ♠ 42
♡ 972
◇ J4
♣ Q109876

Bid 2 ♣ and later 3 ♣ over 2 ♠, 2 ♡ or 2 ◇ as sign off.

The Stayman convention was originally part of the Acol System but is widely played with the 2 Clubs System. It is wise to agree on it before starting to play.

Weak No Trump

A one NT opening bid here implies a balanced hand of 12–14 points. As the opening hand is weaker more is needed to support but you still operate on the basis that 25 points combined will be enough for game. Therefore: 0–10 points. Pass unless holding a long suit, in which case you can make a weak take-out. 11 points. Raise to 2 NT. 12 points or more. Raise to 3 NT. Jump bids (1 NT–3 ♠ or 3 ♡) are similar and require 12 points at least. Use of the conventional response of 2 ♣ (Stayman) is similar but the necessary adjustment must be made due to the weaker opener. The Weak No Trump is popular with club/tournament players, but master your strong No Trump play *first*. Introduce this more skilled play later, when *you* are ready.

Opening Bid of 2 No Trumps

This is a standard range of 20–22 points and balanced shape. Raise to 3 NT with 5 points or over.

Response of 3 ♡ or 3 ♠ asks partner to raise to game in the suit if he holds three cards; otherwise to bid 3 NT. In other words a response of three in a suit is constructive and not a weak take-out. A reply of 3 ♣ (Stayman) is asking for a major suit of four cards and works in the same way as 2 ♣ in reply to 1 NT. Some players use the 3 ♣ reply to ask for any four card suit, but this method is more complicated and has many disadvantages. It is better to adhere to the simple method.

Opening bid of 3 No Trumps

This is a gambling type of bid and is based on a long solid minor suit with not much outside, e.g.

♠ 7 6
♡ J 2
◇ A K Q J 9 8 7
♣ 10 9

If doubled (see page 11) you can retreat to your long suit, but in the meantime you may have created difficulties for the opponents. This bid is more associated with the Acol System and it is probably wisest to avoid using it until you have had a fair amount of experience.

Prepared Club

Certain hands present a problem if you have agreed to play the strong no trump, where your only biddable suit is spades or possibly hearts. e.g.:

♠ K J 7 2
♡ Q 4 2
◇ A 7 6
♣ K 8 6

If you open 1 ♠ and partner responds in a new suit at the two level you have no good re-bid as 2 NT would promise 15–16 points. In such cases you open 1 ♣ to enable you to rebid cheaply. This is an exception to the principle that a biddable suit should contain at least four cards. The hand does not contain enough points for a strong no trump but it is of no trump shape and you have agreed with your partner to play the strong no trump.

The Prepared Club is purely a makeshift device, a convenience. It is not forcing and partner need not reply. It need not be employed if partner has already passed as you are no longer compelled to respond. Occasionally it is necessary if you are playing the weak no trump, for example, if you have 15 points and your four card suit (a major suit) is too weak to be biddable.

No Trumps Quiz

1. Which of the following qualify for the opening bid of 1 NT (15–17)

(a) ♠ KJ762
♡ AQ6
◇ K2
♣ A97

(b) ♠ K 10 3
♡ AQ8
◇ KJ 10 7
♣ AQ2

(c) ♠ KQ2
♡ K 10 8
◇ AJ976
♣ K8

(d) ♠ 3
♡ AQ43
◇ KJ98
♣ AK86

2. Your partner opens 1 NT (15–17) playing the strong no trump and the next player passes. What do you say on

(a) ♠ KJ4
♡ AJ9
◇ J643
♣ 986

(b) ♠ KJ43
♡ Q63
◇ 32
♣ A963

(c) ♠ J98432
♡ 63
◇ 10942
♣ 8

(d) ♠ 63
♡ 86
◇ AKQ 10 7 6
♣ 762

(e) ♠ AJ843
♡ K42
◇ K62
♣ 32

3. Your partner opens 1 NT (12–14) playing the weak no trump and the next player passes. What do you say on

(a) ♠ Q742
♡ KJ62
◇ Q 10 8
♣ 10 3

(b) ♠ AJ6
♡ KQ2
◇ A976
♣ 10 7 2

(c) ♠ KQ 10 6 2
♡ A2
◇ QJ65
♣ 42

(d) ♠ AJ72
♡ 3
◇ KQ86
♣ K543

Answers to Part Two No Trumps Quiz follow on the next page.

Answers to No Trumps Quiz

1. (a) No. 5 card major. Open 1 ♠.
   (b) No. 19 points. Open 1 ◇.
   (c) Yes. 5 card minor is all right.
   (d) No. Singleton spade. Open 1 ♡, 1 ◇ or 1 ♣.
2. (a) 3 NT. 10 points guarantees 25 combined.
   (b) 2 ♣ Stayman – asking for four card major.
   (c) 2 ♠. Weak take – out.
   (d) 3 NT. Don't bother with the diamonds.
   (e) 3 ♠. Forcing.
3. (a) No Bid. You cannot afford 2 ♣ as you cannot revert to 2 NT if partner says 2 ◇.
   (b) 3 NT. 14 points is enough for game.
   (c) 3 ♠. Forcing.
   (d) 2 ♣. Stayman. Raise rebid of 2 ♠ to 4 ♠. Otherwise bid 3 NT.

RE-BIDS BY OPENER AND RESPONDER

Re-bid by Opener

The opener's first bid at the level of one can vary to the extent of being between 10 and 19 points. It may be an evenly divided hand or may comprise one or more long suits. The first re-bid should clarify the position.

1. After Limit Response (see page 31). If partner has responded 1 NT (6–9 points) the opener will only rebid if he thinks he can improve the contract, e.g. Opening bid 1 ♠, Response 1 NT;

(a)	(b)	(c)
♠ A K 10 3	♠ A K 9 7 6 2	♠ A K 8 6 5
♡ K Q 7 5	♡ K 10 6	♡ K 10 3
◇ J 2	◇ J 7 5	◇ A 6
♣ J 8 3	♣ 2	♣ K 10 9
No Bid.	2 ♠.	2 NT.

On (a) the combined total cannot exceed 23 and may be only 20 points so that game is not possible. As the hand is balanced leave it at 1 NT.

(b) is an unsuitable hand for 1 NT and will be safer in 2 ♠ with a six card suit.

On (c), a good hand, 23 combined points are certain and 25–26 are possible. Bid 2 NT and if partner has 8–9 he should bid 3 NT.

Following a reply of 2 NT (11–12 points) opener can either pass with a minimum and suitable shape, or raise to 3 NT with spare values. With an unbalanced hand he can rebid his suit at minimum level as a sign off, or he might bid game, e.g. after 1 ♠ opening – 2 NT reply:

(d)	(e)
♠ K Q 10 8 6	♠ K J 10 9 7 5
♡ A 5 4	♡ 3 2
◇ A 7 5	◇ A Q 8
♣ Q 7	♣ J 5
Bid 3 NT.	Bid 3 ♠. (Sign off.)

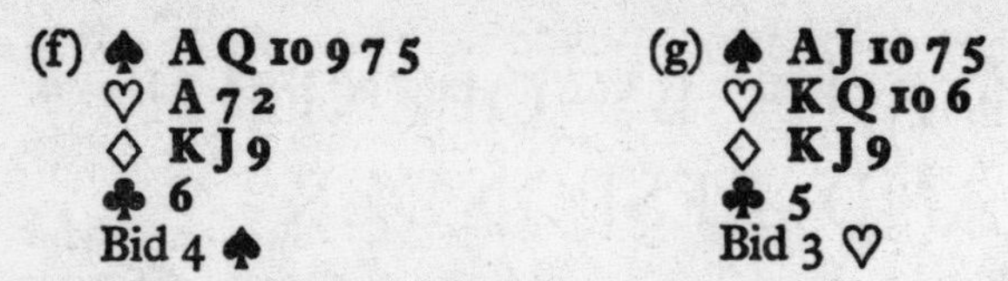

On (g) partner must only raise 3 ♡ to 4 ♡ if he is holding four trumps. He should give preference to 3 ♠ with three and appreciate that the opener is not keen on no trumps.

After a response of 3 NT opener will usually pass unless he has a long suit, in which case he bids four in it.

After a simple raise (1 ♡–2 ♡) opener will usually pass unless holding 17–18 points, or 7 probable tricks in his hand, when he can jump to 4 ♡. A re-bid of 2 NT implies a balanced hand of 17–18 points and a 4 card suit. A bid of 3 in a new suit is termed a 'trial bid' and suggests that partner may be able to bid game if he has a good raise and some help in the 'trial' suit. E.g. after openning 1 ♡–2 ♡ reply:

(a)	(b)	(c)
♠ 6 4	♠ 4 2	♠ 4 3
♡ A Q J 7 5	♡ A Q J 9 8 6	♡ A Q J 9 5
◇ K Q 8	◇ A K 7 2	◇ K 10 8 6
♣ Q 8 6	♣ 4	♣ A Q
No Bid.	Bid 4 ♡.	Bid 3 ◇.

On (c) you hope partner will convert to 4 ♡ if he has a good raise with some high cards (e.g. Q J) in diamonds. If he says 3 ♡ you pass.

Following a double raise (1 ♡–3 ♡) you are likely to bid game if there is any hope at all, but you are justified in passing if your opening is minimum or you lack aces. If your points are largely made up of queens and knaves the opponents can probably win four tricks before you get in.

After an immediate raise to game (1 ♡–4 ♡) you will be right to pass in the vast majority of cases as partner's hand is mainly distributional and not loaded with points.

2. After Non-Limit Response. If partner responds with one in a higher ranking suit he may have as little as 6 points, but may have a good opening bid. You are obliged to re-bid unless your partner has previously passed.

A re-bid of 1 NT shows a balanced hand but outside your agreed range for an opening bid of 1 NT. That is to say you have a no trump type of hand which you did not open as such because it did not qualify.

Thus, if you are playing a strong no trump the re-bid of 1 NT = 13–15. If playing weak no trump the re-bid will show 15–16. A re-bid of 2 NT = 17–18 points and 3 NT = 19 points.

These figures are based on the fact that you need about 23–24 points to play in 2 NT, just short of game. If your partner only promises 6 you need 17–18 to bring the total up to the required figure.

A re-bid of one in a higher ranking suit guarantees no additional strength, e.g. 1 ♣–1 ♡–1 ♠. Opener is merely showing two suits and has not increased the contract. Nor does the re-bid of a second suit at the two level, provided that it is lower in rank than the original suit called. e.g.:

S.	N.
1 ♡	1 ♠
2 ◇	

South as opener does not indicate any extra strength than he would if he had re-bid 2 ♡. North can return to 2 ♡, but may prefer to leave 2 ◇. A single raise of partner's suit is not strong but should include four trumps. A double raise is invitational and indicates about 16–17 points. A jump to game would need 18–19 points. These figures can be reduced if the opener's hand is strong in distribution.

If partner bids two in a lower ranking suit he has increased his side's commitment and his minimum is therefore raised to 8 points. With less than 8 and a suit lower in rank than your partner's opening bid, call 1 NT as being the cheapest available bid.

Following a response at the two level opener can rebid 2 NT with 15–16 points and 3 NT with 17–18. This is due to the fact that the partner's share of the necessary 25 is greater, leaving less for the opener to find.

After a forcing to game jump bid (1 ♡–2 ♠ or 1 ♡–3 ♣) (see page 32) the opener should re-bid more or less as he would have done had the bidding been a level lower. e.g. after opening 1 ♠–3 ♣ reply:

(a)	(b)	(c)
♠ A Q J 9 5	♠ A J 10 8 6	♠ A Q J 9 6 4
♡ K 4 2	♡ K J 10 8	♡ A 7 5
◇ Q J 3	◇ A 9 4	◇ 2
♣ 7 3	♣ 6	♣ K J 6
Re-bid 3 ♠	Re-bid 3 ♡	Re-bid 3 ♠

Hand (c) is very strong and is likely to make a slam, taking 12–13 tricks. But there is no need to rush it. A jump bid in a forcing situation shows a completely solid suit and not much outside.
e.g.: 1 ♠–3 ♣. Opener holds:

♠ A K Q 9 8 6 4 ♡ 7 4 ◇ K 8 ♣ 3 2	Re-bid 4 ♠. (Game).

Re-bid by Responder
If the responder has limited his hand by bidding either no trumps or raising partner's suit, he need not take further action unless forced or invited to do so. For example if opener makes a jump rebid (1 ♠–1 NT–3 ♡) he must bid again. If opener raises a response of 1 NT to 2 NT responder is expected to bid again if he is in the upper bracket, ie. 8 or 9 as opposed to 6–7. Or if the opener changes the suit after a response of 2 NT e.g.

S.	N.
1 ♠	2 NT
3 ♡	

responder must carry on. He must not bid 4 ♡ with less than four trumps. He should show preference for 3 ♠ with three and only reluctantly bid 3 NT if most of his strength is in minor suits.

If responder has changed the suit (1 ◇–1 ♡ or 1 ♠–2 ♣) his hand may vary to a large extent. Broadly speaking he can bid on if he has reasonable values in excess of what he has shown. E.g. if South opens 1 ♡, North replies 1 ♠ and South re-bids 2 ♡, North would then reply:

(a)	(b)	(c)
♠ A J 7 4	♠ A J 7 2	♠ A 10 7 2
♡ 4 3	♡ K 4 3	♡ Q 3
◇ K 7 6 4	◇ K 10 9 6	◇ K 10 8 6
♣ 10 8 6	♣ 6 3	♣ Q 10 7
No Bid.	Bid 3 ♡.	Bid 2 NT.

With (a) you have nothing to spare. With (b) you hold 5 points more than you indicated so far and you have K x x opposite your partner's suit which you know is longer that four as he re-bid it. With (c) you have 5 points more than you said.

In judging how high to bid follow the yardstick that an opening bid facing another opening bid should produce a game if the hands fit. In other words, if your partner opens the bidding and you can fairly say that, had you been dealer, you would have opened, game is likely. It is not purely a matter of points. If each of your hands comprises a distributional opening bid and the hands fit, game is quite likely even though you do not hold the vital 25 points. The total of 25 points is far more accurate with no trump bidding, where distributional factors and ruffing (trumping) do not arise.

Re-bid Quiz

1. With neither side vulnerable you open 1 ♠ and partner responds 1 NT. What do you say on

(a) ♠ K Q J 9
♡ K 6 4
♢ A 7 4 3
♣ J 9

(b) ♠ A Q J 10 9 7
♡ A K 8
♢ K 2
♣ 3 2

(c) ♠ K J 9 7 4
♡ K 10 8 6
♢ A Q 4
♣ 2

What would you re-bid if partner had responded 2 NT?

2. South opens 1 ♡ and North responds 2 ♢: South re-bids 2 NT. What should North say on

(a) ♠ 7 3
♡ 4 2
♢ A K Q 10 8 6
♣ J 4 3

(b) ♠ 4 2
♡ Q 8 6
♢ A Q J 9 5
♣ Q 10 6

(c) ♠ 6 4 2
♡ 5 3
♢ K Q 8 6 4
♣ K 7 5

Answers to Part Two Re-bid Quiz follow on the next page.

Answers to Re-bid Quiz

1. *Response* 1 *NT*. (a) No Bid. Too few points for game and a suitable hand for 1 NT.
   (b) 3 ♠. Seven playing tricks plus a king. You have 7 playing tricks as you should make 5 out of your 6 Spades, plus 2 tricks in hearts. You also have the King of diamonds which may win a trick. Game is still possible if partner's 1 NT is above 7 points.
   (c) 2 ♡. Shows no extra strength but offers a choice of two suits. 1 NT unsafe with singleton club.
   Response 2 *NT* (a) 3 NT. 14 plus 11 points = 25.
   (b) 4 ♠. You expect to make 4 ♠ so bid it. 3 ♠ would be a sign off.
   (c) 3 ♡. Not keen on no trumps. Inviting preference to 3 ♠.
2. (a) 3 NT. You can provide six tricks. No point in re-bidding 3 ◇ which would be a sign off. All your diamonds are likely to win tricks because the AKQ will draw out the knave.
   (b) 3 ♡. Forcing. You are prepared to go beyond 2 NT and if partner holds a five card heart suit you wish to be in 4 ♡. If he has only four hearts he should bid 3 NT. You cannot hold more than three hearts.
   (c) No Bid. You have just your 8 points and not a particularly good suit.

OPENING FORCING BIDS

The necessity for an opening forcing bid (i.e. a bid to which partner is compelled to reply) arises when a player is so fortunate as to hold a hand with which he thinks he can make game without any material help. 'Why', you may ask 'does he not just bid game?' Firstly because he may not be able to judge which suit to call or whether to bid no trumps. Secondly, because there might be a chance of a slam. Consider these hands –

West		East
♠ A K Q 10 6	N	♠ 7 5 3
♡ A K 5 4 3	W E	♡ 8 6 2
◊ 2		◊ 9 7 6 3
♣ A 4	S	♣ 8 6 5

Assume that the remaining cards are divided in a normal manner and that West plays with spades as trumps. If he leads out his top spades the knave will probably fall, giving West five tricks. If he plays out his hearts he will lose the third round and make altogether four tricks and the ace of clubs will make ten. If spades were trumps it would be wise to play only three rounds to start with and retain at least one for an emergency.

West will have made ten tricks, enough for game, but if he opens 1 ♠ East cannot possibly make a bid and game will be missed. It may take a round or two of bidding to find the best contract and to ensure that the bidding does not stop too soon, the opener's partner must co-operate to the extent of ensuring that he keeps the bidding open until game is reached. If the second player bids, partner (in this case East) need say nothing as the bidding must get back to West. Otherwise East *must* bid. The conventional opening forcing bid is 2 ♣.

(a) Negative Response is 2 ◊ (cheapest available bid as 2 ♣ is conventional). This denies either an ace and a king, or 8 points including at least one ace or king.

(b) Positive Response. Bid either a reasonable suit or 2 NT

with a balanced hand. If your suit is diamonds reply 3 ♢, as 2 ♢ is negative.

After his negative reply, responder should next show a 5 card suit on the second round or support his partner. If he can do neither he bids 2 NT.

Reverting to the example above the bidding would proceed:

West	East
2 ♣	2 ♢
2 ♠	2 NT
3 ♡	3 ♠
4 ♠	

West tries his second suit (hearts) but East should give preference to the first suit so that West can then bid game.

Another example –

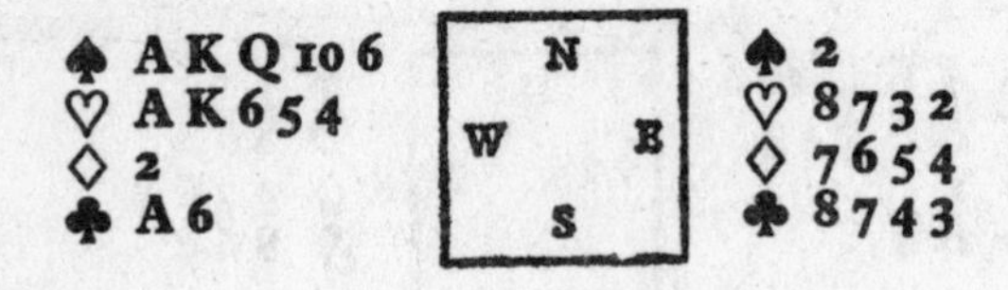

Bidding –

West	East
2 ♣	2 ♢
2 ♠	2 NT
3 ♡	4 ♡

Here East's hand only appears to have any value when West bids hearts. The final contract is sound but it has taken a little time to reach. It was only reached because East manfully kept the bidding open.

Of course, partner will not always have such a bad hand as the ones shown. They have been purposely made out hopeless to indicate the type of hand that qualifies for an opening bid of 2 ♣.

The qualifications are:

(1) A balanced hand containing 23 points or more
(2) A hand with 4½–5 quick tricks which can reasonably expect to take at least nine tricks.

With a balanced hand of 23 points the opener will re-bid 2 NT following a negative reply of 2 ♢. With 25 points opener re-bids 3 NT.

In the Acol System the partner is permitted to pass a re-bid of 2 NT with a hopeless hand of less than 3 points.

In the 2 Clubs System the proviso whereby a re-bid of 2 NT can be passed by partner does not necessarily apply and a 2 ♣ bid is forcing to game in all cases, except by partnership agreement.

Opening Bids of Two other than 2 Clubs

As 2 ♣ is used for all hands that are capable of making game single-handed it is possible to use openings of 2 ♠, 2 ♡ or 2 ◇ as strong intermediate bids. In the Acol System these are described as showing eight or more playing tricks with a good 6 card suit. Partner is expected to respond once to give the opener another chance, 2 NT being the negative.

(1) Single raise. Trump support with a sure trick outside. Most players expect an ace.

(2) New Suit at same level. (e.g. 2 ♡–2 ♠). Reasonable 5 card suit with one trick, e.g.

♠ A J 10 6 4
♡ 4 2
◇ 6 3 2
♣ 8 6 2

Respond 2 ♠ to 2 ♡.

(3) New suit at 3 level. Requires about 8 points as the bidding has been raised. e.g. opening bid 2 ♠, bid 3 ♡ on

♠ 4 3
♡ A Q 10 7 5
◇ K 4 3
♣ 7 6 2

(4) Double Raise in Opener's suit. Shows good trump support but denies an ace or void.

(5) Jump in new suit (2 ♡–3 ♠). Shows solid self-supporting suit with no losers (A K Q x x x x) or A K Q J x x

(6) 3 NT. Balanced 11–12 points. Will not contain two aces.

In the 2 Clubs System an opening bid of 2 ◇, 2 ♡ or 2 ♠ may be made on a strong hand based more on points and is not completely forcing. It is probably more satisfactory to employ the Acol type bid, but in any case it is wise to agree on the point with a strange partner.

Two Bid Quiz

1. Partner has opened 2 ♣ and the next player passes. What do you say on

(a) ♠ A K 10 6 2
♡ 4 3 2
♢ 9 7 6
♣ 5 4

(b) ♠ J 5 4 3 2
♡ K 7 5
♢ Q 10 8
♣ 7 6

(c) ♠ 4 3
♡ J 4 2
♢ A K J 8 6
♣ 8 7 6

(d) ♠ K Q 6
♡ 10 8 7
♢ K 9 7 5
♣ 6 5 4

(e) ♠ 4 2
♡ 8 7 6 4 3 2
♢ 3
♣ 9 7 6 2

2. Partner has opened 2 ♡ (forcing for one round) and the next player passes. What do you say on

(a) ♠ 3 2
♡ A J 5
♢ K J 8 2
♣ 10 9 8 7

(b) ♠ J 4 2
♡ 3
♢ J 7 6 4 2
♣ 8 7 6 4

(c) ♠ A K Q 10 8 7 6
♡ 3
♢ 10 8 6
♣ 7 4

(d) ♠ A Q 8 6 4
♡ 3 2
♢ J 3 2
♣ 8 4 2

Answers to the Part Two 2 Bid Quiz follow on the next page.

Answers to Two Bid Quiz

1. (a) 2 ♠. Positive reply. Biddable suit with A and K.
   (b) 2 ◇. Negative reply. Only 6 points. If opener rebids 2 NT, bid 3 ♠ next round.
   (c) 3 ◇. Positive response. You must bid 3 ◇ as 2 ◇ would be negative.
   (d) 2 NT. Balanced hand. 8 points with 2 kings.
   (e) 2 ◇. Negative response. Bid hearts next round.
2. (a) 3 ♡. Positive response. Trump support.
   (b) 2 NT. Negative response.
   (c) 3 ♠. Solid suit.
   (d) 2 ♠. Sufficient to bid new suit at the same level.

OPENING PRE-EMPTIVE BIDS

These are purely defensive bids at the level of three or higher designed to make it difficult for the opponents to enter the bidding safely or to be able to interchange information with their partner with sufficient accuracy to reach a satisfactory contract.

Consider this hand –

♠ K Q 10 9 8 6 4
♡ 2
◇ J 10 8 7
♣ 3

With only 6 points you have not got a proper opening bid. Nevertheless, if spades were trumps you would take about 6 or 7 tricks. With another suit as trumps you would take barely any.

If the opponents hold the balance of strength and are given a free run they will probably reach their best contract. But if you put up a barrage they may find it impossible.

Suppose you are South, dealer, and hold

♠ 7
♡ A J 9 7 6
◇ K 6 3
♣ A Q 8 7

You would open 1 ♡ and wait to hear what partner said. But suppose that East, on your right, dealt the hand and bid 3 ♠; then what do you do? You cannot really risk 4 ♡ and you might miss game if you pass. You have a problem.

Defence against Opening Bids of 3

(1) Overcall with a strong suit (at least 6 cards).

(2) Make a conventional call asking partner to bid his best suit. There are various alternative conventional calls for this situation but these two are fairly satisfactory.

(a) Bid 3 NT.

(b) Lower Minor. This means bid 4 ♣ over all opening bids of three except 3 ♣. In this case bid 3 ◇.

(3) Double. Penalties. Implies you expect to defeat the contract. You should have strength in the opponents' suit. High cards in other suits are unreliable as they may be trumped.

Qualifications for Pre-Emptive Bids

(1) 7 card, or longer, suit.

(2) Little high card strength. About 8 points maximum. Less than two defensive tricks (tricks you expect to win even though the opponents are playing the contract in *their* selected suit or in no trumps).

(3) No four card major suit other than the one bid.

(4) Reasonable hope of taking six tricks if not vulnerable, or seven tricks when vulnerable (being vulnerable was explained on page 11). As you do not expect to make the contract and your bid is purely defensive to prevent the opponents making the best of their hands, you must not risk too big a penalty.

Action by Partner

In view of the known weakness of the opening bid partner will usually pass.

With three or four quick tricks he can raise partner to game, even with only one trump. The important thing is to hold aces and kings that will win either the first or second round of a suit.

Only respond 3 NT with a good fit in partner's suit as you will not be able to get into his hand, i.e. it will not be possible to win a trick in his hand to enable you to continue playing his long suit. This aspect will be explained later in the section on play, page 93 et seq.

SLAM BIDDING

A slam involves bidding and making either twelve or thirteen tricks. In other words you can only afford to lose one. If you achieve this you are entitled to a good bonus. The awards can be found on the scoring table, page 122. Slams can be considered likely in the following instances –

(1) Where the combined total of points is 34. In this event the opponents can only hold 6 points (2 kings or 1 ace and 1 queen).

(2) After a forcing to game jump bid, where the opener is strong and would have forced had his partner opened. e.g. South opens 1 ♠ and North responds 3 ♢. South holds

♠ A K J 9 6
♡ K 4 2
♢ K 8 4
♣ K 6

If North had opened 1 ♢ South would have forced with 2 ♠.

(3) If partner opens and makes a jump re-bid and you hold a full opening bid. As an opening bid facing an opening bid will usually produce game, an opening bid with jump, opposite an opening bid should produce more than game.

(4) After a positive reply to an opening 2 ♣.

If you decide to bid a slam the most important cards are aces. It is no fun to bid, say, 6 ♠ and follow suit while the opponent plays off two aces. There are various ways of finding out about aces but the most popular method is the Blackwood Convention.

Blackwood Convention

When the bidding has indicated that a slam is possible and it is firmly established which is to be the final trump suit, a bid of 4 NT is conventional and asks partner to state the number of aces he holds.

Response

5 ♣ = No ace or, all four aces.
5 ♢ = One ace.
5 ♡ = Two aces.
5 ♠ = Three aces.

With no ace it is natural that you should make the cheapest reply possible, hence 5 ♣. If partner has only two aces himself he will realize that a slam is not possible and will go back to five of the agreed suit. If a player with all four aces bids 5 ♣ it means that his partner who has initiated the slam investigation has none. It is hardly possible for neither player to hold an ace.

If the reply to 4 NT confirms the fact that all the aces are jointly held, a bid of 5 NT asks about kings and the responses are much the same:

6 ♣ = No king.
6 ♢ = One king.
6 ♡ = Two kings.
6 ♠ = Three kings.
6 NT = Four kings.

Cue Bids

A bid in a new suit at a high level when a suit has already been agreed as trumps is a cue bid and shows first round control. e.g.

South	North
2 ♠	3 ♠
4 ♣	

South says, in effect, 'When we play eventually in spades I can take the first trick if a club is led as I will either put on the ace or I will trump it'.

Similarly, suppose over 2 ♠, West overcalls with 3 ♢ and North bids 3 ♠. If South next bid 4 ♢ he would imply the same message with diamonds. He could not possibly want to play the hand in his opponent's suit. Besides, spades have already been agreed as being the suit that will eventually be trumps.

DEFENSIVE BIDDING

A player who makes an overcall or intervening bid is at a disadvantage compared with his opponents insofar that he has no knowledge of the type of hand his partner will be able to provide.

On the other hand, the opponent on his left who has heard his partner open the bidding may well be able to judge that his own cards, together with what he may expect from his partner, may be sufficient to defeat the intervening bid. In such a case he may well double, which means that if the contract is defeated the resultant penalty is increased, more so if the declarer is vulnerable, having already made one game. These factors alter the basis on which an overcall is assessed. Instead of judging the issue on points it is more important to consider how many tricks you expect to make if you are left in.

There are several reasons for making a defensive overcall.

(1) To make a contract for your side, either part score or game.

(2) To harrass opponents and upset their bidding machinery.

(3) To indicate a sound lead for your partner if the player on your left becomes declarer.

(4) To pave the way for a cheap sacrifice against the opponents. That is to say, you may, by outbidding the opponents prevent them scoring game at a fairly economical price.

In making an overcall you should estimate that you will at least succeed in making within two tricks of your contract if vulnerable, or three tricks if you are not vulnerable. This means that if you are doubled the penalty will not exceed 500 (either 200 + 300 vul: or 100 + 200 + 200 not vul:).

Some hands containing as many as 13 points do not qualify as a sound overcall, while others with perhaps only 6 or 7 are perfectly good. The following principles are given as a guide:

(a) Never overcall on less than a 5 card suit. At the two level you should have a 6 card suit.

(b) The suit should be a good one that you can lead out from your own hand without undue loss.

(c) The suit should be one that you are prepared for partner to lead.

(d) Hesitate to make an overcall where much of your strength is in the opponent's suit. In such cases your hand is more useful in defence.

Examples –

Love All. South opens 1 ♡ and you are the next player to call.

(a)	♠ A Q J 9 8	(b)	♠ Q 3
	♡ 5 3		♡ K 10 8 6
	◇ 6 3 2		◇ K J 9 7 3
	♣ 10 8 7		♣ A 5
	Overcall 1 ♠.		No Bid.

On hand (a) your spade suit is quite good and a spade lead is welcome. If you pass North might bid 2 NT and be raised to 3 NT, and partner will be unlikely to lead a spade as he will not be aware of your strength in the suit. The question of opening leads is considered in detail in the section on defensive play, page 69.

On hand (b) you have a broken suit of diamonds that would suffer badly if you had to lead it from your own hand. Your strength in opponent's suit (hearts) makes the hand more valuable in defence and if you stay quiet they will probably go down (be defeated).

Informatory Double

You may sometimes be confronted with a hand containing about 13 or more points that has no 5 card suit, yet provides good support for any suit other than the one opened. It seems a pity not to be able to compete and the problem is how best to set about it. The solution is to make an informatory or take-out double.

So far the term 'double' has always implied that you do not expect your opponent to fulfil his contract and that by doubling you expect to extract a larger penalty. This holds good, particularly at high levels and in certain other instances (see below).

But suppose South deals and bids 1 ◇, then you, West, can double with the following in mind. Namely, how often could you hold a hand with which you could genuinely expect to defeat a contract of only one diamond? Remember your partner, so far, has had no opportunity to bid and you have no idea what he has. Short of a freak deal, there could be no such occasion. And therefore a double in such circumstances is treated as conventional. It asks your partner to respond in his best suit.

Put briefly, the double of a suit call at the level of one or two, when partner has not yet bid, is informatory and requests partner to bid his best suit no matter how weak. e.g.

South opens 1 ♢ and you, West, hold

(a)		(b)	
	♠ K Q 9 6		♠ A 10 8 6
	♡ A Q 7 4		♡ K J 9 8
	♢ 3 2		♢ 2
	♣ A J 3		♣ K 10 9 8

In each case you double. You are prepared for partner to bid any suit and hope he will choose a major. One way of looking at it is this. If you feel that it is better that partner selects the suit as you might pick the wrong one, you double.

The amount of strength required is about 13 points or more, but the distribution must be taken into account. If you have three cards in opponents' suit you have three 'passengers' and only ten cards left to support your partner.

In hand (b) you have only one card in their suit and consequently twelve active cards; this justifies you in doubling on only 11 points as you are quite happy whatever suit your partner calls.

You need to be a little stronger if you double 1 ♠ than, say, 1 ♣, as your partner is forced to reply with two of a suit over 1 ♠, but need bid only one of a suit over 1 ♣.

Action by doubler's partner

If the third player passes, the doubler's partner is compelled to bid and should call his best suit at the cheapest level. e.g.:

West doubles 1 ♢ and North passes. East holds –

(a)		(b)	
	♠ 10 7 4 2		♠ A J 9 8 6
	♡ 4 3		♡ K 6 5
	♢ 6 5 4		♢ 7 3
	♣ Q 8 7 6		♣ Q 10 8
	Bid 1 ♠.		Bid 2 ♠.

Hand (b) is quite a bit stronger than hand (a) so it would be misleading to make the same bid. Bidding 2 ♠ shows about 8–11 points and invites support but is not forcing. If there is an intervening bid there is no obligation for the doubler's partner to speak as the double no longer stands and the bidding will go round to the doubler again anyway. In other words the double is superseded by the subsequent bid. But you would still bid with a reasonable hand. With hand (b) above, substituting low cards for the king of hearts and queen of clubs it would be correct to call 2 ♠ if North bid 2 ◇ after West, your partner, has doubled 1 ◇.

Action by Opener's Partner

After the opening bid has been doubled the only strong bid available to the opener's partner is re-double. This term has not so far cropped up. It is the counter to a double. If you bid up to 4 ♠ and I think I can defeat you I can double (for penalties).

But if you are totally confident of making the contract you may re-double. If you are successful your score is doubled up again; the original 120 becomes 480 plus 50 bonus for making the re-doubled contract. If you fail the penalty is proportionately increased.

In the present stage of the bidding re-double is still a gesture of confidence but it is unlikely to remain undisturbed because a contract of, say, 1 ♠ re-doubled would be game if made ($2 \times 30 = 60, 2 \times 60 = 120$).

Re-double, after the opening bid is doubled, promises about 9 points or more, but not necessarily support for partner's suit. It carries the message 'We have the better hands and should make a score. Either we will make a contract of our own or double our opponents for penalties when they retreat'.

Apart from re-double, any other bid is purely defensive and is designed to obstruct the doubler's partner. Thus if after South has opened 1 ♡ West doubles and you are North with:

(a)	(b)	(c)
♠ 3 2	♠ 3 2	♠ K J 9 6
♡ Q 10 8 6	♡ K 9 8 6 4	♡ 4 2
◇ K 7 4 2	◇ K 10 7 4	◇ A J 8 6
♣ 7 3 2	♣ 7 3	♣ Q 10 3
Bid 2 ♡.	Bid 3 ♡.	Re-double.

A bid of a new suit need not be strong but should be playable and contain 5 cards. A bid of 1 NT shows about 7–8 points balanced.

Action by Doubler's Partner after Re-double.

After the opener's partner has re-doubled, the next player, on the right of the opener, is not compelled to bid at all. However, he should try to help his side by making a cheap bid. E.g. after

South opens 1 ♡ and West doubles, and North re-doubles, East holding –

(a)		(b)
♠ 8642		♠ 43
♡ 63		♡ 7642
◇ 9742		◇ 8765
♣ 732	but	♣ 943
Bids 1 ♠.		Passes.

Jump Overcalls (1 ♡–2 ♠) show a good suit and about seven playing tricks. They are not forcing. An overcall of 1 NT needs to be strong (16–18 points) including at least one stopper in opponents' suit. It is risking a large penalty to overcall 1 NT on a moderate hand.

If the opponents' hands are known to be limited in strength it is permissible to compete with less than the strength recommended above. E.g. South opens 1 ♡ and the next two players pass. It is safer for East to call now as the opponent on his right cannot hold more than about 5 points.

Penalty Doubles

A double is considered to be for penalties whenever partner has made a bid. Also, doubles of contracts at the level of three or higher are generally regarded as penalty.

Doubling contracts at the two level often produces good results as the overcaller has little knowledge of what is against him. Care must be taken as an unsuccessful double may present the opponents with game. But if you hold two probable tricks in the opponents' suit with a trick outside and not more than two cards in your partners' suit, a double is likely to succeed. With good support for partner's suit you are better advised to raise him.

Doubling high contracts is more dangerous as the opponents are better able to judge their values the longer the bidding goes on. Therefore to double a game or slam that has been freely bid is likely to lose more than it will gain.

Even if you hold two aces against a small slam in a suit you must not double. Either the opponents have made a mistake or they haven't. If you make both your aces you should be satisfied to score 50 when you never expected to score at all. The risk if you doubled is if one opponent is void in a suit and the small slam is made. Because then you present your opponents with a further 230 points. If they re-double your loss is much worse.

Defensive Bidding Quiz

1. At Love All South opens the bidding with 1 ♢. You are West. What do you say on –

(a) ♠ A K J 9 8
♡ 4 3
♢ 10 8 6
♣ J 4 3

(b) ♠ 4 3
♡ J 7 6 4 2
♢ K J 9 8
♣ A 6

(c) ♠ K 10 8 6
♡ A J 9 8
♢ 4 3
♣ A J 9

(d) ♠ K J 9
♡ A Q 8
♢ K J 9 7
♣ K 10 9

(e) ♠ 6 3
♡ K 8 6
♢ A Q 10 8 6
♣ Q 10 4

(f) ♠ A K Q 10 8 6
♡ 4 3
♢ 7 6
♣ A J 9

2. With East–West vulnerable, South, your partner, opens 1 ♡ and West doubles. What do you say on –

(a) ♠ 4 3
♡ Q 9 7 6
♢ K 10 7 2
♣ J 3 2

(b) ♠ A J 9 7
♡ 3 2
♢ K 10 8 6
♣ Q 8 5

(c) ♠ Q J 10 9 4 3
♡ 2
♢ J 7 2
♣ 8 6 4

(d) ♠ K 9 6
♡ 9 4 3
♢ K 7 4 3
♣ Q 10 8

Answers to the Part Two Defence Bidding Quiz follow on the next page.

Answers to Defensive Bidding Quiz

1. (a) 1 ♠. A suit you want led. You are not risking a big penalty by overcalling.
   (b) No Bid. A bad suit and you are strong in opponents' suit.
   (c) Double. Asking partner for best suit.
   (d) 1 NT. Strong, with good cover in their suit.
   (e) No Bid. Hope they go on in diamonds.
   (f) 2 ♠. Strong overcall. Not forcing.
2. (a) 2 ♡. Defensive.
   (b) Re-double. 10 points. No promise of heart support.
   (c) 1 ♠. A playable suit. Not forcing.
   (d) 1 NT. 8 points. Balanced hand.

PART THREE

PLAY
THE DEFENDERS' GAME

The Defenders' Game

Note: In the Play Section, the play of a card will be indicated by first the symbol of the suit followed by the number of the card. Thus ♠ 5 means the 5 of spades; ♣ K = king of clubs etc. As soon as the bidding has finished and the final contract has been established, the play period starts. The player on the left of the declarer makes the opening lead.

The Opening Lead Against No Trumps

In defending against a no trump contract the main object must be to establish a long suit against declarer. If you can lead out a card to which no-one else can follow suit your card must win.

If your partner has bid it is almost invariably correct to lead his suit, as a suit that he has bid is probably better than your own. The mere fact that the opponents have called no trumps over it is no justification for not leading it.

In most cases you lead the top of partner's suit. But if you hold 3 or more cards headed by an honour you lead a low card in order to preserve an honour behind the declarer. Example:

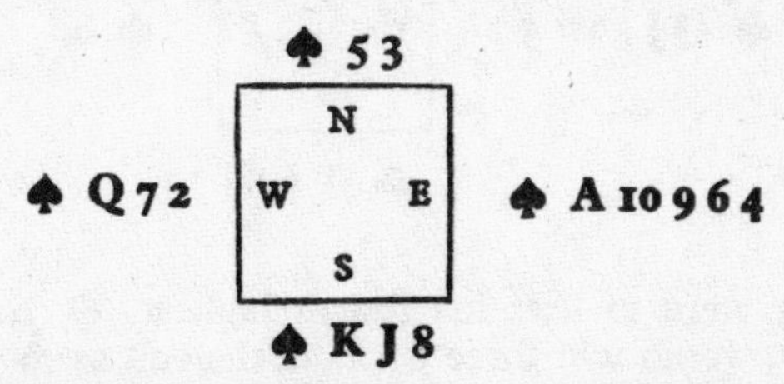

South is declarer in no trumps after East has bid spades. If West leads ♠ Q, South will take two tricks, but if West leads

♠ 2 and East plays ♠ A, South will only make one. East can appreciate that his partner has not led his highest spade, for if that were the case South would hold K Q J 8 7 which would hardly be consistent with the bidding. If your partner has not bid it will in most cases be best to lead your own longest. If your suit is headed by a sequence you lead the top card. Thus from:

Q J 10 7 6 lead Q
J 10 9 7 6 lead J.

If the third card is one step removed from the second you may still treat it as a sequence, e.g.

from K Q 10 9 7 lead K
from Q J 9 6 4 lead Q.

The reason that you lead the top of a sequence is this. Suppose you hold Q J 10 7 6 3 and lead the queen which forces out the king, when you regain the lead you play knave which drives out the ace. Now your ten has become a winner and probably the others also. You can afford to lead a valuable honour if you have an adequate replacement.

Suppose, however, your suit is not so solid. Now you lead the fourth highest card. This is the fourth card from the top, e.g. from K 10 8 6 3 lead the six. You cannot consider leading the king, because you have no replacement, your next best card being the ten. Some people consider it right to lead fourth highest always, but this does not apply if you have a sequence. Consider this position –

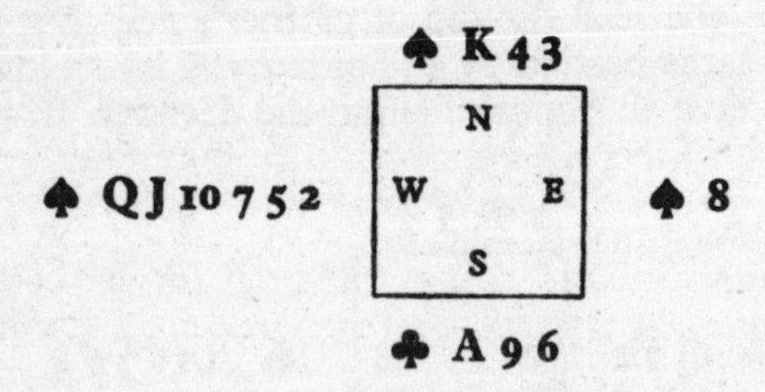

If West were to lead his fourth highest, ♠ 7, South, with dummy, would win three tricks in the suit as ♠ 9 would take the first.

To lead your longest suit is correct in most cases as you are hoping to establish it. But if the opponents have bid your suit which consists of, say, Q 8 6 4 2, your chances of making tricks by leading it are very small. In such cases it is best to play an unbid major suit. The reason for this is that the opponents are likely to call a major suit if they are strong in it, whereas they may not necessarily show a minor as game requires so many tricks.

The Opening Lead Against Suit Contracts

Here the alternatives are more varied. If partner has bid it is wisest to lead his suit, again leading a low card if you have three or more headed by an honour. But if you hold the ace of his suit you should lead it as it might later be trumped. If your partner has not bid you have to decide for yourself and the various alternatives are as follows –

(1) *Top of Sequence.* E.g. K Q J, Q J 10 etc. A sound lead as it is constructive and gives nothing away.

(2) *Ace or King* from a suit headed by A K. The advantage here is that you will probably win the first trick and will be in command when you see dummy. You will then be able to decide whether to carry on with your suit or switch to another. In this you will be guided by your partner's play and this aspect of defence will be explained later under Signals.

From a suit headed by A K it is equally correct to lead either the ace or the king. But as the king is also led from a sequence headed by K Q difficulties may be encountered when a player leads the king which may be from either combination. For this reason modern practice favours the lead of the ace from a suit headed by ace and king.

This may also be a convenient moment to illustrate one of the fundamental differences between defending against no trumps and against a suit. Holding A K 7 6 5 against no trumps it would be correct to lead the six (fourth highest) and this is because you are planning on a long term policy. You do not mind giving up an early trick if it means making four later. But against a suit declaration you must try for faster tricks. After two rounds a suit is likely to be trumped and therefore you must lead your ace and king.

(3) If you have no sequence and no suit headed by A K, you still lead fourth highest of your longest suit. But it is bad to lead a low card from a suit headed by the ace. You may lose to a singleton king or you may allow declarer to make an unnecessary trick. E.g.

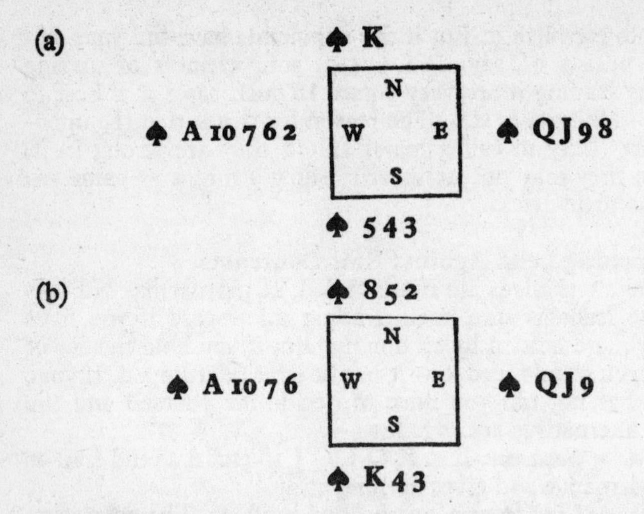

In (a) if ♠ 6 is led, ♠ K wins, and West may never make his ♠ A as it may be trumped.

In (b) if West leads ♠ 6, South, being last to play, will make a trick with his king. It would also be poor play for West to lead out his ♠ A as it would only attract low cards. If West holds on to his spades and waits for the suit to be led to him he may capture South's ♠ K.

There is a common belief that it is a major crime to lead away from a king. There is an element of risk attached, but it may not necessarily be fatal –

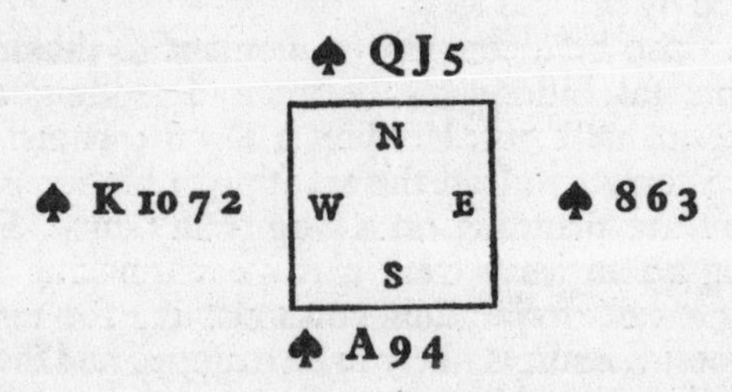

If West leads ♠ 2 and ♠ Q is played from dummy and wins, West has certainly got off to a bad start. But, providing he does not again lead from his king he will still make it. All that has happened is that the king, normally a winner on the second round, has been demoted to the third round.

A lead from a queen or knave is more dangerous.

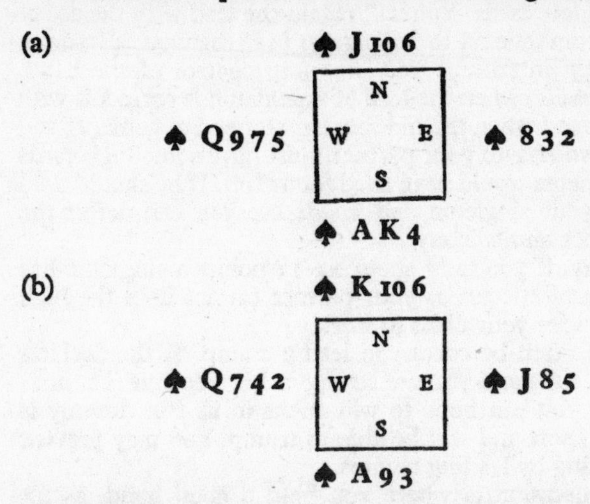

In (a) if West leads ♠ 5 and ♠ 10 wins in dummy, he will never make a trick with ♠ Q which has been relegated to a winner on the fourth round.

In (b) if West leads ♠ 2 and ♠ 6 is played from dummy and East plays ♠ J South will win with ♠ A. By playing ♠ 3 from his hand, South can make all three tricks in the suit, for if West follows with ♠ 4, ♠ 10 in dummy will take the trick. If West puts on ♠ Q it will be taken by ♠ K. East and West would have made a trick between them had they not led the suit.

(4) With none of the more attractive leads available you may elect to lead from three small cards. You are not so much concerned with trying to establish tricks, although you may be successful in doing so, but rather hoping to give as little help as possible to the declarer. With three small cards some players lead 'top of nothing' e.g. from 9 6 4 they lead the 9. This may create problems for the partner who cannot decide whether you hold 2 or 3 cards in the suit. An alternative is to lead the middle card and play the higher one next time. Thus with 9 6 4 lead the 6 and follow up with the 9 next round. This is a convention called M.U.D. as the initials stand for middle-up-down.

(5) The lead of a singleton (one card) or doubleton (two cards) is a gamble that may or may not succeed. The best time

to try such a lead is if you hold some control in trumps, such as ace and two low cards. You will regain the lead with the ace of trumps and can then try to put partner in so that you can trump. With nothing in trumps you may lose control of the hand. Another occasion when the lead of a singleton is correct is with a very bad hand when the bidding has stopped at game. If you hold only two knaves your partner must have some high cards or the opponents would have tried for a slam. If he should hold the ace of your singleton and a side ace you can defeat the game contract immediately.

Conversely, if you hold about 12–13 points a singleton has little chance of success as your partner cannot hold the high cards needed for your plans to work.

(6) It can often be correct to lead a trump. If the declarer has bid two suits and you are strong in his side suit (i.e. non-trump suit) you can hope to win tricks in it. But dummy is likely to be short and will be able to trump. You may prevent this happening by leading trumps.

Another occasion is where you hold a good hand, as for example:

♠ J 10 3
♡ K J 7 5
◇ A 7 3
♣ K 8 6

Declarer on your right opened 1 ♠ and his partner raised to 3 ♠ and declarer bid 4 ♠. As you hold 12 points it is unlikely that your partner will have much, so that the burden of defeating the contract is likely to fall on you. Rather than try to set out to win four tricks you are better off to sit back and hope declarer loses four tricks. In other words you play a passive game, trying to give your opponent as little assistance as possible. You start by leading ♠ 3 (not an honour) in case partner has an honour by itself. Each time you get the lead you play something that gives nothing away.

Had the bidding suggested that any hand held a long suit other than trumps you might have had to make a more aggressive lead in order to try and build up four tricks before the opponents had time to discard their losers on the long suit.

Signals

With dummy exposed the declarer (who, as explained on page 14, plays dummy's hand) is in a better position in that he can see his partner's cards and can manipulate them to the best advantage. Although the defenders can also see dummy, their own hands are concealed. In order that the defending side can make the best use of their material it is necessary that they should co-operate, using established methods of signalling to indicate whether to continue with a certain suit, or switch to another, and, if so, which.

Most common of the signals is the high–low play, sometimes referred to as a 'peter', to indicate a desire for a suit to be continued. Two possible reasons for wanting partner to carry on with his suit are one, that you can win the third round with a high card, or two, that you have only two cards and will be able to trump. Here are two examples. It is assumed that spades are trumps –

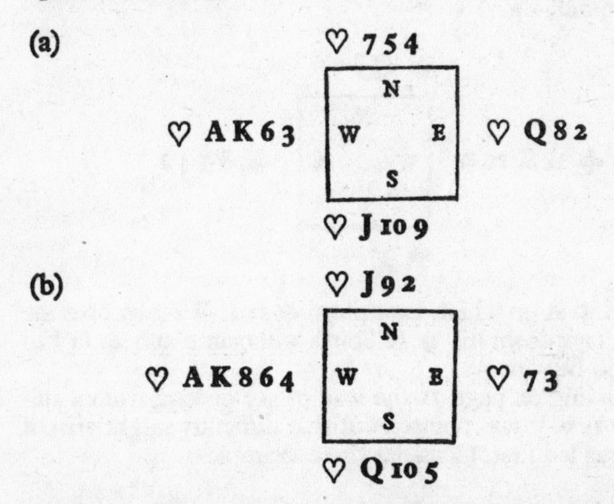

On hand (a) West leads ♡ A which implies probable possession of the king. East plays ♡ 8 because he hopes to take the third round with ♡ Q. Had he held ♡ 8 7 2 he would have played ♡ 2 as he had no reason to think that a continuation of the suit will be beneficial. On hand (b) East plays ♡ 7 on ♡ A. West continues with ♡ K and notices his partner's play of ♡ 3, completing a high–low signal. He carries on and East ruffs (i.e. trumps) the third lead which would otherwise have been won by the ♡ Q in South's hand.

A card is considered encouraging if it is roughly 6 or over. More accurately it should be described as a card that *can be identified as not being your lowest.* If your partner leads an ace or other high card that you cannot beat the natural inclination is to toss on it your lowest card. If, therefore, you are noticed to play a card that is *not* your lowest it is logical that you should be trying to convey a message.

If you are dealt 9 2 it is very convenient as your 9 will register. But if you have 3 2 all you can do is to play 3 to the first trick and hope partner is alert, realizes that the 2 has not appeared and comes to the conclusion that you are starting a high–low signal.

Just as the play of a relatively high card is an encouragement to carry on, similarly the play of a low card is a warning. Signals are not unlike traffic lights and if your partner plays, say, the 2 it is a red light. You should stop unless you are sure of your ground, e.g.

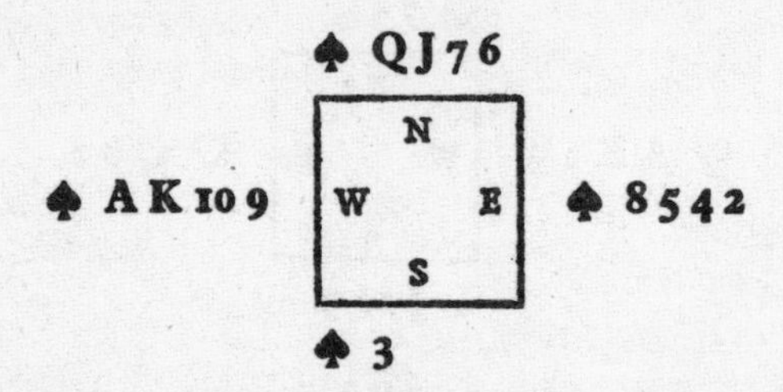

West leads ♠ A on which East plays ♠ 2. If West ignores the signal and lays down his ♠ K South will trump and ♠ Q J in dummy will be winners.

In discussing on page 71 the lead of ace or king from a suit headed by A K it was pointed out that difficulty might arise if the king was led first. Consider these examples:

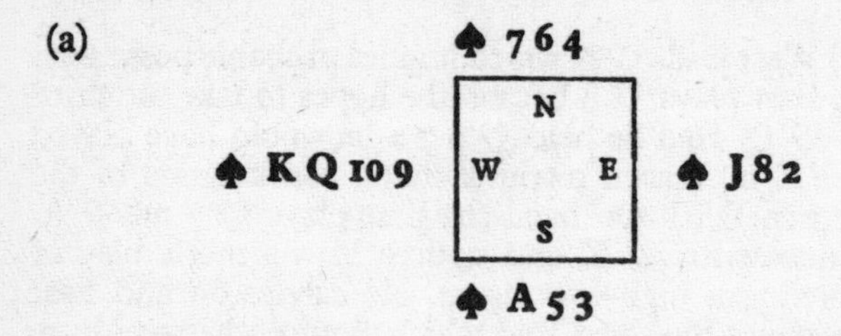

(b)

On hand (a) West leads ♠ K. If East should play ♠ 2 and South plays ♠ 3, West should switch to another suit because South may have played ♠ 3 holding ♠ A J 3 and be hoping to lure West into carrying on with his suit and fall into a trap. But on hand (a) East should play ♠ 8 as his ♠ J is a valuable card if his partner holds ♠ K Q.

On hand (b) if ♠ K is led it would be wrong for East to play ♠ 8 for in this case West would next play ♠ A and South would make a trick with his ♠ Q later. But if East plays ♠ 2 and West switches to another suit, South's ♠ Q will be captured later by ♠ K. If the lead of K is liable to be either from A K or K Q it is almost impossible for East to know what to do. That is why it is recommended that with a suit headed by A K the ace is led.

It is justifiable to start a high–low signal with the knave, especially if the other card is very low. Holding J 2 you play the knave first for if you play the two partner will assuredly stop.

But it is not usual to 'peter' with the queen. In fact, if partner leads the ace of a suit (A from A K) the play of the queen is a conventional way of indicating the knave, so that partner can play a low card on the next round to pass the lead to you. The queen could be the only card you hold in that suit in which case you would trump next time.

Another common form of signal is the discard of a high card to indicate the suit you would like partner to lead when he has the chance. For example, if spades are trumps and the diamonds are distributed as follows –

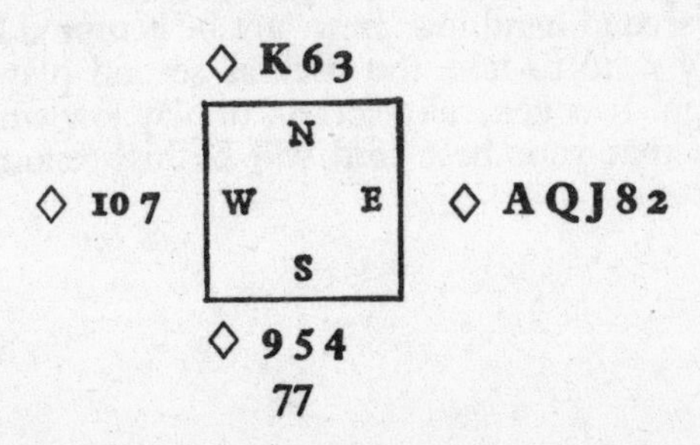

South leads out trumps (spades). East cannot follow suit and discards ◇ 8. This tells his partner to lead a diamond when he gets in. Suppose South is declarer in no trumps and West has succeeded in establishing his long suit (spades) and has 2 or 3 good cards to lead out when he obtains the lead. Apart from his spades West holds ♡ A 9 2. At the first available opportunity he should discard ♡ 9, a high card telling his partner which suit to lead if he gets in and cannot return a spade.

General Principles

There are certain precepts relating to defensive play that are apt to be laid down without any particular reason being given. They are given the appearance of government regulations. Basically they are sound but it is necessary to know the reasons.

1. Second Player Plays Low

If you are second player, your partner is fourth and last. Therefore he will be able to judge more easily whether to play a high card or a low one. Consider the following example –

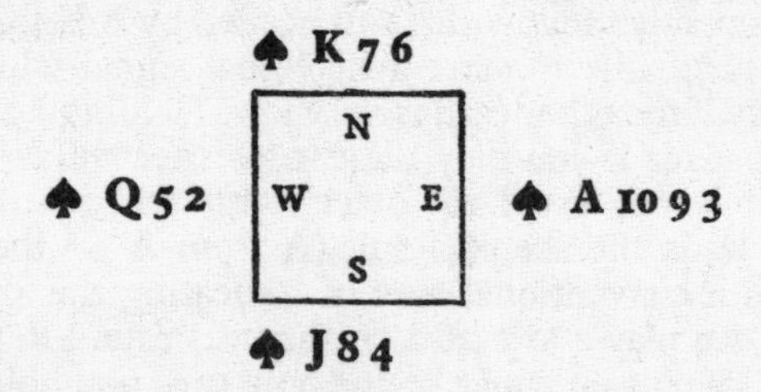

South, needing to make a trick in spades, leads ♠ 4. There can be no point in West playing ♠ Q 'to force out ♠ K'. If ♠ 7 is played from the table East can surely beat it. If ♠ K is played East will either be able to win with ♠ A or play a low and useless card if he has not got ♠ A.

But 'second hand low' must not be accepted blindly. If you urgently need to take the trick as second player you should play high. It is generally correct to play low when you cannot be sure that your best card will be high enough to win the trick. But –

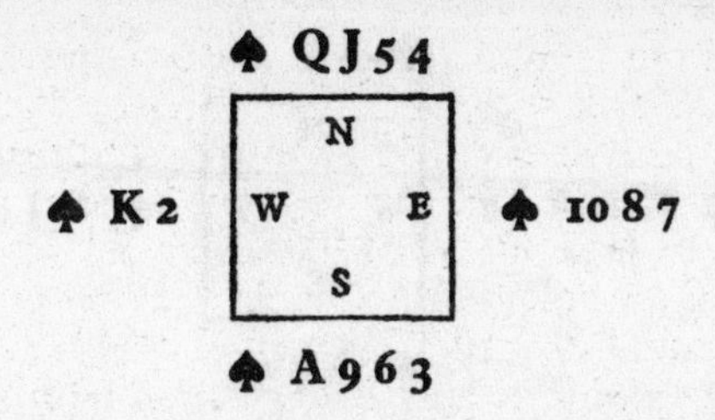

South leads ♠ 3 from his closed hand towards ♠ Q J 5 4 exposed in dummy. You are correct to play ♠ K second in hand because your card will take the trick. Moreover, if you play low and your partner does not hold ♠ A, your ♠ K will fall next time to the ace.

2. Third Player plays High

If the first two players have contributed small cards it is logical that you should play high in order that you may try and win the trick. If it does not win, your high card may dislodge a big card from declarer and thus assist your partner. For example, South is declarer in a no trump contract and West leads his fourth highest heart, his longest suit –

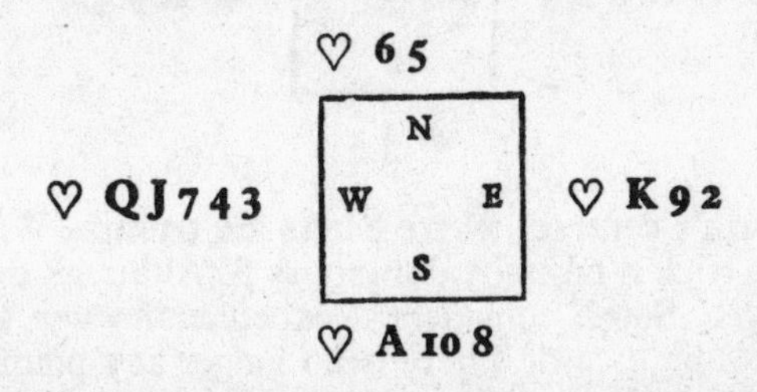

Dummy plays ♡ 5 and you, as East, must play ♡ K. If South takes this with ♡ A you may be sad to lose your valuable king, but you have succeeded in promoting your partner's Q J to winning cards and if your side can regain the lead you will win four more tricks in hearts. Suppose you had played ♡ 9 on the first round, declarer would win with ♡ 10 and still hold ♡ A to control the suit.

In playing high as third player it is correct to follow with the lower of cards of equal value and in sequence. The reason for this principle will be clearer with this example –

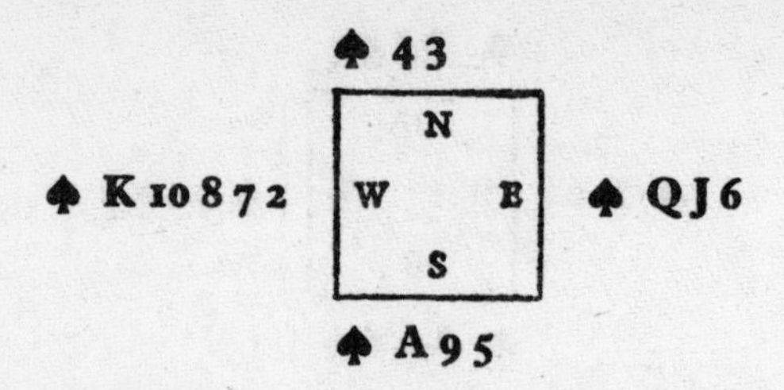

Against South's contract, either in a suit or no trumps West leads ♠ 7 and dummy plays ♠ 3. If East plays ♠ J and South wins with ♠ A it is clear to West that East also holds ♠ Q, for otherwise why should South use his ace when he could have taken ♠ J with ♠ Q? But if East follows with ♠ Q and South wins with ♠ A West cannot draw the same conclusion as it needed ♠ A to win against ♠ Q. In fact, if West thinks his partner has played correctly he will assume that South holds ♠ J. Of course, if dummy has taken the trick, the third player will not waste a high card. –

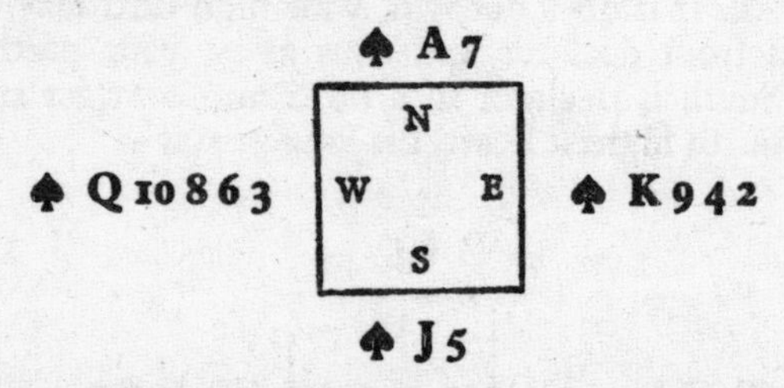

Against South's contract where hearts are trumps, West leads ♠ 6 and the trick is taken by dummy ♠ A. Although dummy is second player, South considers it expedient to win the trick and plays his high card. There is no longer any point in you, East, playing ♠ K as you would have done had ♠ 7 been played from the table. You would, however, be right to play ♠ 9, a high card, as a signal to partner that you hold a strong card in the suit he led (see Signals page 74).

It is not always necessary to play your highest card, particularly when there is an honour in dummy –

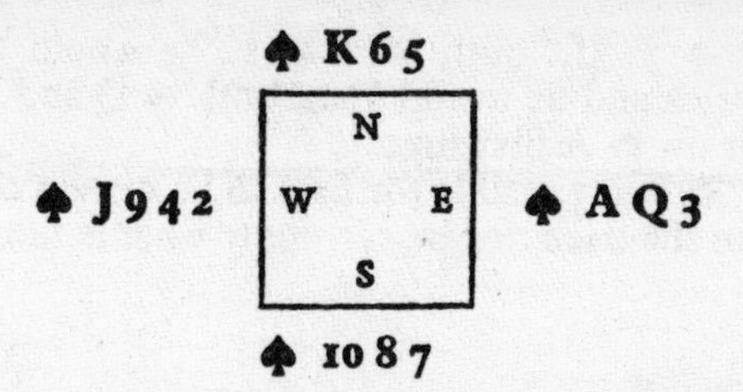

West leads ♠ 2 against South's contract in hearts. When ♠ 5 is played from the table you can play ♠ Q (not ♠ A) as this is the lowest card able to take the trick. This is a fairly obvious case but in the next example the purpose of not playing your highest card is to retain an honour card over dummy.

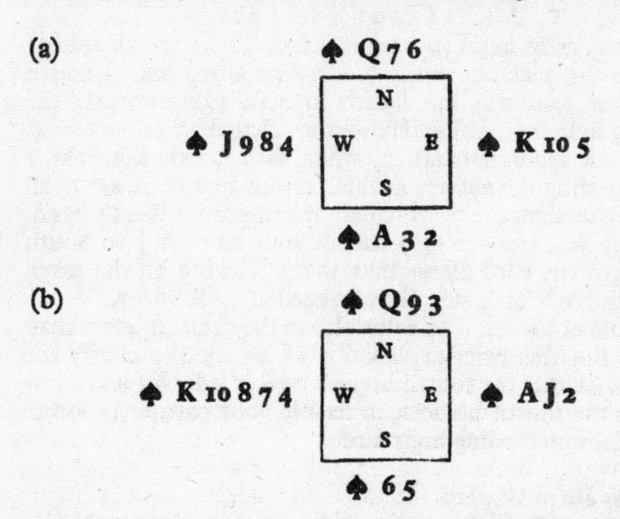

Against South's contract in no trumps West leads ♠ 4 on hand (a). When ♠ 6 is played from the table East should play ♠ 10. This is not his highest spade but he wishes to keep ♠ K sitting over ♠ Q. If he plays ♠ K and it is taken with ♠ A, South will later make ♠ Q also. Supposing South had held ♠ A J 3 and West ♠ 9 8 4 2 and led ♠ 2, East's ♠ 10 would be taken with ♠ J but with ♠ K placed over ♠ Q South would make only two tricks instead of the three he would win had ♠ K been played, giving South ♠ A, ♠ J and ♠ Q.

On hand (b) if ♠ 3 is played on the opening lead of ♠ 7,

East plays ♠ J. If South held ♠ K he would always have made one trick and he would make both ♠ Q and ♠ K if East were to put up ♠ A first time.

In hand (b) it is possible for East to be certain that ♠ J will actually win the trick, for he can apply what is termed the rule of eleven.

Rule of Eleven

If a card led can be assumed to be the fourth highest card held in the suit, by subtracting the value of the card led from eleven, the balance remaining represents the number of cards *higher* than the one led which are distributed between the remaining three hands.

Suppose you set out all the cards in one suit viz.

A K Q J 10 9 8 7 6 5 4 3 2

and assume, as in hand (b) that 7 is led. There are altogether 7 cards in the pack above the 7. Of these three must be with West as his lead was the fourth highest. Consequently the remaining four are missing. Hence the calculation 11 — 7 = 4.

Now back again at hand (b) when ♠ 7 is led. You take 7 from 11, getting the answer 4 which means that there are in all 4 cards *higher* than the 7, which are missing from West's hand. In dummy you can see Q 9 and in your hand A J so South cannot have any card *higher* than the 7. Ticking off the cards that are visible West's suit must be headed by K 10 8 7.

The Rule of Eleven is of value also to the declarer as we shall see later. But this brief explanation of it may also clarify the earlier advice that the fourth highest card is led. Not just a low card, but the fourth highest, to enable your partner to locate some of the outstanding high cards.

3. Leading Up to Weakness

This is a logical expression for it means that you put the declarer into the position of having to judge how high a card he should play as second player.

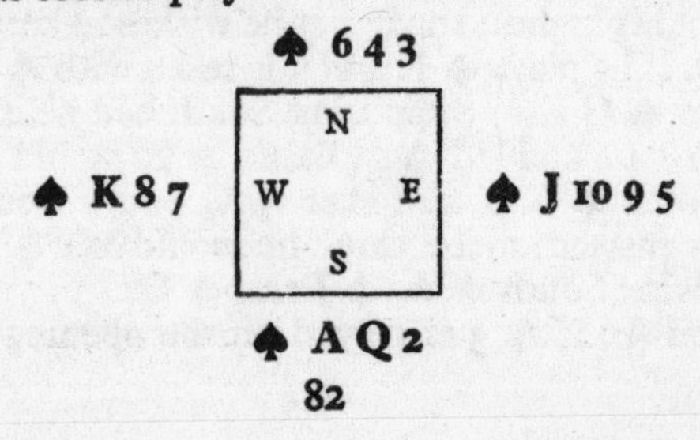

If East leads ♠ J South can see that dummy is incapable of winning the trick. He has to guess whether to make certain with the ace or try his luck with the queen. If East held lower cards, e.g. 10 6 4 2 it would be correct to lead a low card to the weak suit in dummy.

4. Leading Through Strength

This is the natural companion to leading up to weakness as it may compel declarer to play a high card if second player in the hand. It is safer to advise leading through short strength. If dummy holds A J 10 6 5 in a suit it would be dangerous to play through it as you will merely establish the suit and very likely trap your partner's queen in the process. Consider the following

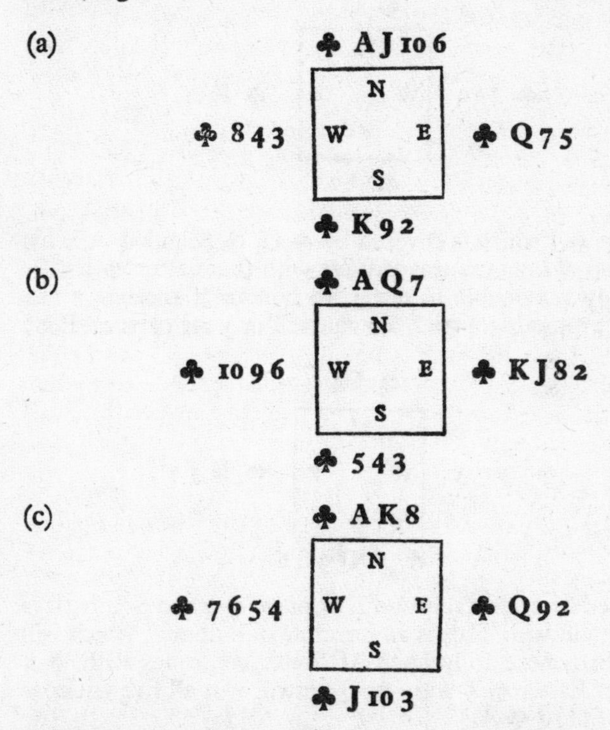

In hand (a) if West leads a club and South plays dummy's ♣ 10 it will not matter whether or not East plays his ♣ Q as the defenders are most unlikely to win a trick anyway. In hands

(b) and (c) a club lead by West is safer as East can hardly hold an honour that can be trapped.

A reasonable principle is to avoid leading through strength in dummy that is missing more than one of the top honours.

5. Covering an Honour with an Honour

The basic principle for covering an honour with an honour is that when two or more high cards fall together the lower ones left in become promoted, For example, the queen will normally take a trick on the third round after the ace and king have been played. If, however, the king is led and taken by the ace, the queen moves up and becomes the highest card on the second round.

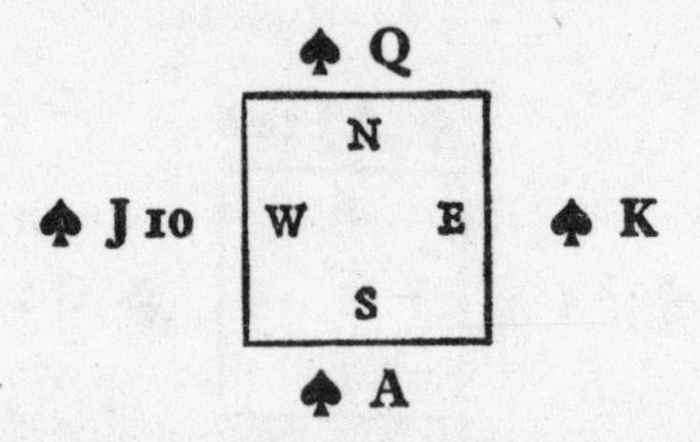

West leads ♠ J which is covered by ♠ Q, ♠ K and ♠ A. This clean sweep of honours leaves West with the master ♠ 10.

It is only reasonable to cover an honour if there is a fair chance of promoting a trick for yourself or your partner. E.g.:

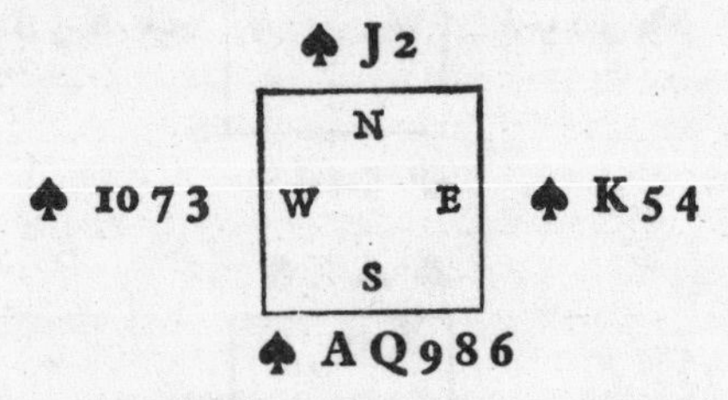

If ♠ J is led from the table and East plays ♠ 4 and South plays ♠ 6, ♠ J will win. This is an example of a finesse, which will be described more fully later. If South continues with ♠ 2 and covers East's ♠ 5 with ♠ Q he will win all five tricks as ♠ K will fall to ♠ A.

But consider what happens if East covers ♠ J with ♠ K. He will lose it when South puts on his ♠ A. The next round will be taken by ♠ Q and this will leave West's ♠ 10 as a winner.

Of course, East could not know that his partner held ♠ 10, but he stood to gain by covering. If there is no possibility of gaining a trick, do not cover, e.g.

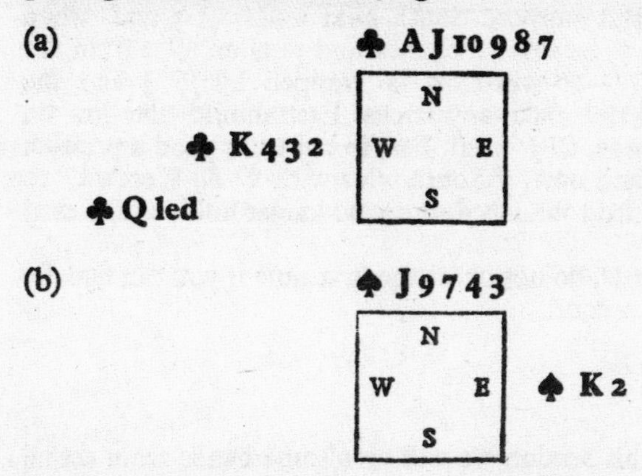

In hand (a) South in no trumps leads ♣ Q. There can be no point in covering with ♣ K as all dummy's cards will be winners. You must hope that South holds only two clubs at most and will be unable to keep leading the suit.

In hand (b) South has opened 1 ♠ and North has raised to 4 ♠ – the final game contract. South enters dummy by winning a trick with, say, ♡ A, and then leads ♠ J. East must not cover because South must hold 4 or 5 spades and West cannot hold anything that might become a trick. It is still unlikely that East will make a trick in spades unless South plays ♠ A, hoping that ♠ K is single in West's hand. But if he does, then East's ♠ K becomes a winner. If you play ♠ K on ♠ J there is a risk that partner holds ♠ A or ♠ Q alone and it falls on your king.

A further example, showing where it is wrong to cover the first time is this –

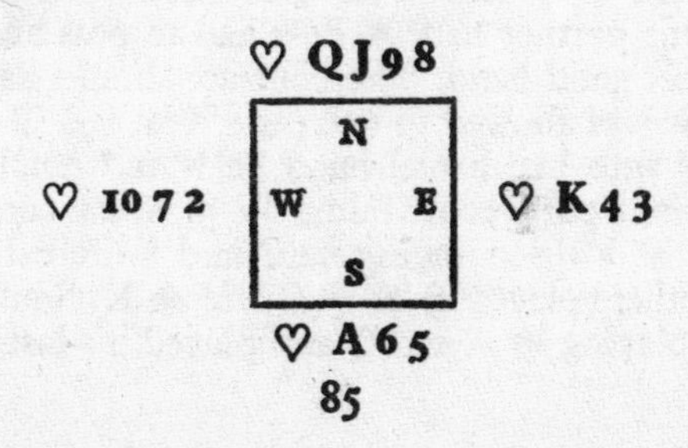

South leads ♡ Q from dummy. Suppose East covers with ♡ K and South wins with ♡ A. To an extent East has achieved his purpose in that his partner's ♡ 10 could be a winner on the third round. But suppose South next leads ♡ 5 and, when West plays ♡ 7, he takes a chance and puts on ♡ 9 from the table, West's ♡ 10 will now be trapped by ♡ J and the defenders will not make any tricks. East should play low on ♡ Q. If this wins, ♡ J is led. East is in just as good a position to play ♡ K, and now, if South wins with ♡ A, West's ♡ 10 will take the third round as dummy no longer holds a high card in the suit.

In other words, do not cover the first time if you can equally well cover the second.

To conclude this section we will give some hands from actual play illustrating defensive plays.

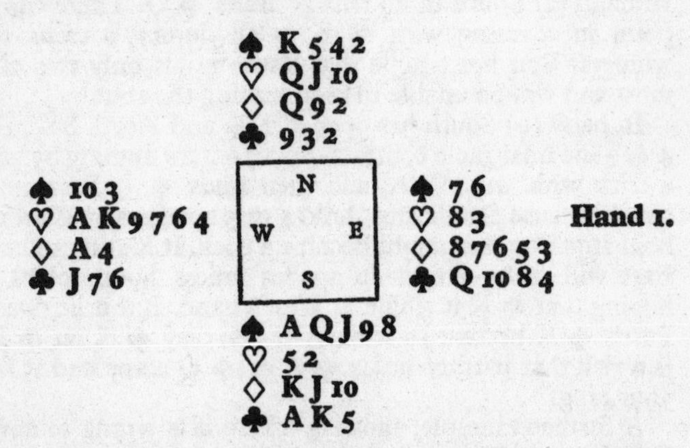

South opened 1 ♠ and West overcalled with ♡ 2. North supported his partner to 2 ♠ East had to pass and South bid 4 ♠ with his good hand. The contract should have been defeated but it was allowed to succeed. West led ♡ A and East, feeling that with his dismal hand he would not be playing a very important part, contributed ♡ 3. West correctly interpreted this as a discouraging card and switched to ♣ 6, to which the others played ♣ 2, ♣ Q and ♣ K. South next drew trumps by playing ♠ A and Q and played his last heart which

West won with ♡ K. West returned a club forcing ♣ A, leaving South with the losing ♣ 5. But South was able to get into dummy with ♠ K and lead the good ♡ Q on which he discarded ♣ 5. He lost a third trick to ◇ A but make ten tricks.

East was at fault. When he played ♡ 3 he was telling his partner it was unsafe to carry on with that suit. He would have played ♡ 3 if he had held ♡ 8 5 3. In that case, if West thoughtlessly plays out ♡ K, South would trump, having no more hearts and ♡ Q would be established as a winner.

The correct play by East was ♡ 8. West would next lead ♡ K and East completes the high–low signal with ♡ 3. West continues the suit and East trumps ♡ Q with ♠ 7 and South overtrumps with ♠ 8. But there is now no chance to discard ♣ 5 on ♡ Q and declarer must lose four tricks.

In the next example South made his contract of 4 ♠ although there appeared to be four certain tricks for the defenders. The reason why these four tricks failed to materialize was that a suit was blocked. That is to say, a player had a winning card that he was unable to play owing to the fact that it was his partner's lead and his partner had no more of that particular suit.

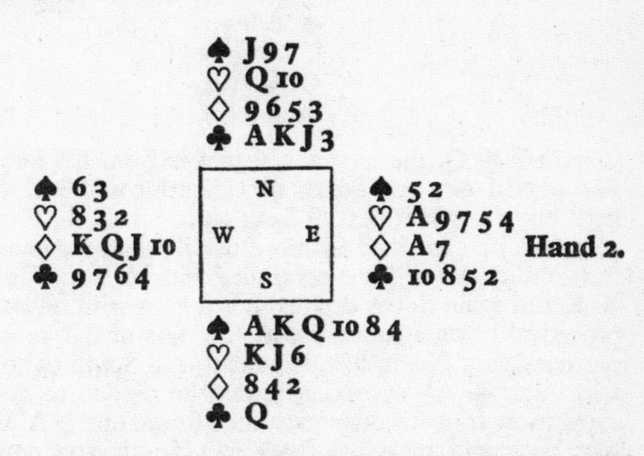

Against the 4 ♠ contract West led ◇ K, top of the sequence, and East played ◇ 7. West continued with ◇ Q and East had to play ◇ A. Having no more of the suit to lead, he laid down ♡ A but that proved to be the last trick for the defence. South took the next trick with ♡ Q. After playing two rounds of trumps he was able to discard his losing diamond on one of dummy's high clubs.

Although it might appear grossly extravagant to take your partner's king with your ace there are occasions when it is necessary. This is such an occasion. Because of the high lead ♢ K East knows that his partner holds ♢ Q and possibly also ♢ J. If he takes the first trick with his ♢ A and returns ♢ 7 to ♢ Q, he can, if necessary, trump the third round. As it is, West will play ♢ J on ♢ 7 and lead ♢ Q. On this East should discard ♡ 9, a clear signal for West to lead a heart.

A similar position occurred on this hand played by South in 3 NT.

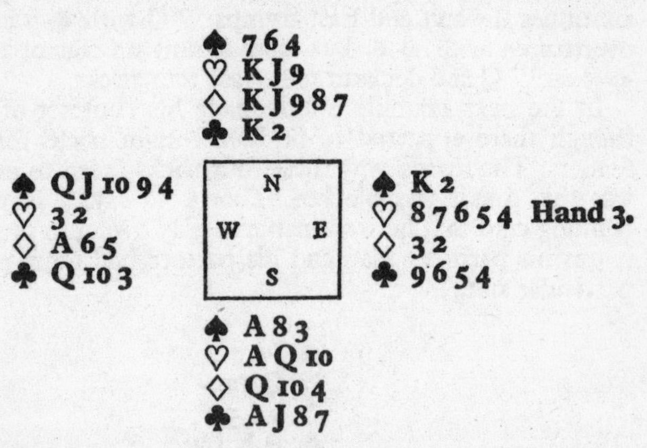

West led ♠ Q, the top of a sequence from his longest suit. East played ♠ 2 and South ♠ 3. South could have taken the trick but thought it best to hang on to his ♠ A. This type of play will be explained in more detail when we consider the tactics of declarer. West continued with ♠ J and East played ♠ K and again South decided not to part with his ♠ A. This proved to be an astute move as East was unable to return his partner's suit. He, in fact, led a club and South (who took the trick with ♣ A), appreciating that he needed to make some extra tricks from his diamonds, then forced out ♢ A. West won that trick and played a spade but South was now in full control.

East, again, should have played ♠ K on ♠ Q to get out of the way.

This would have enabled his partner to clear his suit, having driven out South's ♠ A. When he regained the lead with ♢ A,

West would have enough winning spades to defeat the contract.

In general, if partner leads a card of honour rank and you, his partner, hold a higher honour and one other card, play your honour on his. Your partner would not lead an honour card without others in sequence below it so you will not be throwing tricks away by 'unblocking' by putting your high card on his.

Game was made on the next hand when better defence could have defeated it. The position was similar in that the player with the winning cards was unable to play them out. But this time it was not due to his partner blocking the suit but rather because his partner, when he regained the lead, was unable to lead back the suit.

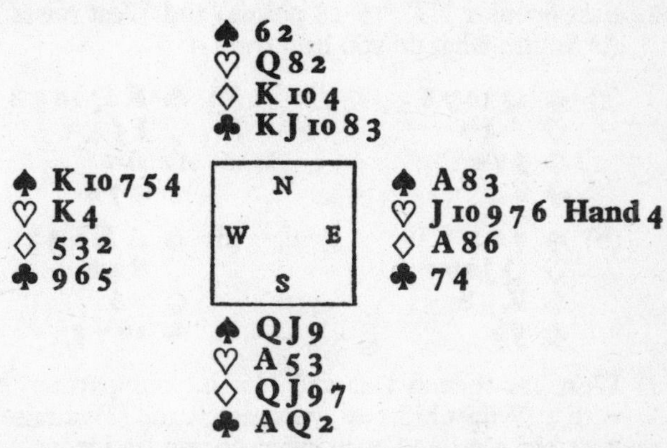

South opened 1 NT (16–18 points) and North raised to 3 NT. West led ♠ 5, the fourth highest of his longest suit. East won the first trick with ♠ A and returned ♠ 8, the highest card of his partner's lead. West captured South's ♠ J with ♠ K and continued the suit, forcing out South's ♠ Q and leaving himself with two winners (10 7).

South played out his partnership's winning clubs and next led ◇ K which East won with ◇ A. Having no spade to return East tried a heart, but South played ♡ A and made the contract with the help of his diamonds.

The defenders had enough tricks to defeat the contract but they were unable to get to them. West held two winning spades but could not play them. The correct play would have been for West to play low on the second round and allow South to take the trick. The effect of this would have been that East, when he got back in with ◇ A, would have still held ♠ 3 to lead back to his partner. South's ♠ Q would have been captured by ♠ K and the remaining spades could have been led out as winners.

If your opponent is sure to make a trick in a suit you are hoping to establish, it is often wise to let him have his trick early in order that you may be able to retain a card of the suit to lead back from the shorter hand. This manoeuvre is called 'ducking' and it is often used for a similar purpose by the declarer as we shall see in the next section.

Defensive Play Quiz

1. East opens 1 NT (16–18 points) and West raises to 3 NT. As South, what do you lead from –

(a) ♠ Q 10 7 6 3
♡ A 4 2
◇ J 7 6
♣ 8 4

(b) ♠ 7 6 2
♡ Q J 10 7 3
◇ K 9 8
♣ 3 2

(c) ♠ K Q 10 9 8
♡ J 5 4
◇ A 2
♣ 9 7 6

(d) ♠ A K 6 4 3
♡ 8 4 2
◇ 7 6
♣ 10 7 3

2. West has opened 1 ◇ and North, your partner, overcalled with 1 ♡ East bid 1 ♠, you passed and West raises to 3 ♠. East bid 4 ♠. As South, what do you lead from

(a) ♠ Q 7 2
♡ Q 9 2
◇ 7 6 4 2
♣ K 8 2

(b) ♠ A 7 4 2
♡ J 2
◇ 9 7 5
♣ J 8 4 3

(c) ♠ 8 5
♡ A 8 3
◇ J 7 2
♣ Q 9 7 4 3

(d) ♠ 9 6 2
♡ Q J 7
◇ J 6 2
♣ A 7 4 2

3. With your side remaining silent, South opened 1 ♠ and North bid 3 ♠. South went on to 4 ♠. Your partner leads ◇ A (leading A from A K). You are East. What do you play to the first trick in each of the following examples?

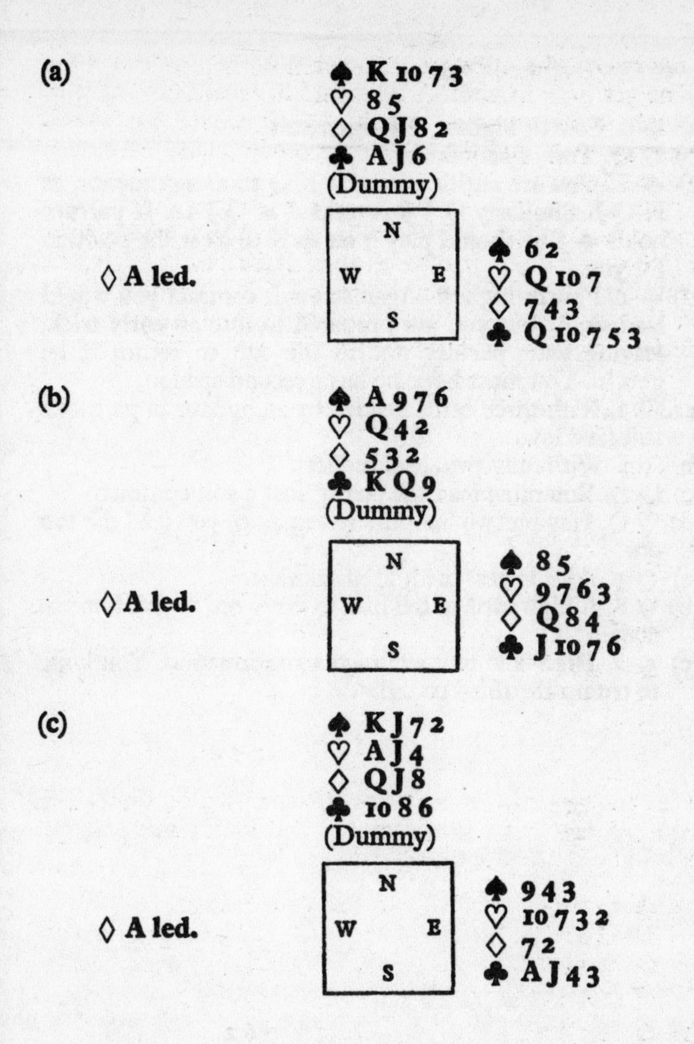

Answers to the Part Three Defensive Play Quiz follow on the next page.

Answers to Defence Quiz

1. (a) ♠ 6. Fourth highest of longest suit.
   (b) ♡ Q. Top of sequence.
   (c) ♠ K. You are entitled to treat K Q 10 as a sequence, as K Q J. Similarly Q J 9 is treated as Q J 10. If partner holds ♠ J he should play it on ♠ K to clear the position for you.
   (d) ♠ 4. Fourth highest. Against a suit contract you would lead ♠ A, but you are prepared to lose an early trick, leaving your partner one in the suit to return if he gets in. You must hope he has a second spade.
2. (a) ♡ 2. With three cards headed by an honour in partner's suit lead low.
   (b) ♡ J. With only two, lead highest.
   (c) ♡ A. You must lead the ace against a suit contract.
   (d) ♡ Q. Having two honours in sequence you lead the top one.
3. (a) ◇ 3. Your lowest card, to discourage.
   (b) ◇ 8. A high card to tell him to carry on, as you hope to make ◇ Q.
   (c) ◇ 7. High–low to encourage a continuation. You hope to trump the third round.

PART FOUR

PLAY

THE DECLARER'S GAME

A. No Trumps

The play of the hand in no trumps is often considered to be more difficult than in suit contracts. This is probably due to the fact that you have less control over the situation. If an opponent leads, the only way you can win the trick is by playing a higher card of the same suit. If you cannot follow suit you cannot take the trick as you do not have the benefit of a trump. This means that you have to take certain measures to retain control.

As soon as the opening lead has been made and dummy has laid down his hand, you should look at your combined resources and assess your chances and make a plan of attack. It is quite logical that you should do your planning at the outset as this is the only time that you hold a full thirteen cards in each hand. If you play hurriedly at the start, you may have a bright idea halfway through, but no longer have the material to carry it out.

First count up your 'top winners'. That is to say count only those tricks that you can make without losing the lead. Usually this total will be below the number you require and this means that you must establish additional tricks. You can do this by forcing out a high card from the opponents. As this will mean losing the lead you have to consider whether you can afford to let in your opponents. It depends on what are called 'stoppers'. These are cards that will take tricks in the suit led by your opponents. The most obvious example of a stopper is an ace because that is a sure winner, but lower combinations of cards will also protect you as we saw in Hand 4 of the previous part on defensive play (page 89).

Consider this example dealt by South –

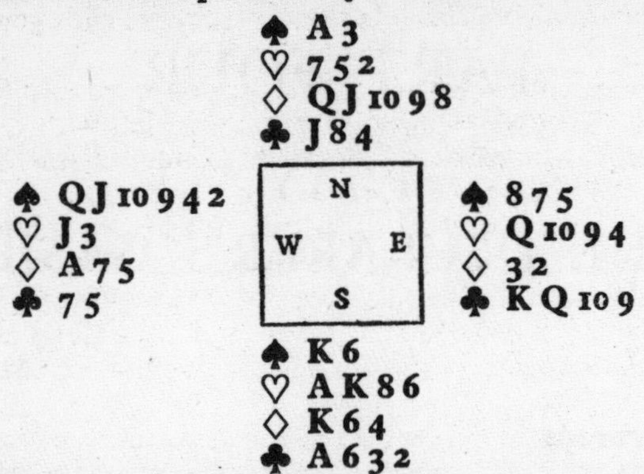

South opened 1 ♡, West overcalled with 1 ♠ and North bid 2 ◇. With 17 points and expecting 8 points from partner, South bid 3 NT. West leads ♠ Q and South stops to count his top winners. There are only 5 and they are ♠ A and K, ♡ A and K and ♣ A. It might be tempting to play those out, but it would not be wise because after taking 5 tricks you would have to lose the lead and the other side would lead out lots of winning spades and clubs. With only 5 sure tricks you need 4 more and this means you must establish a suit. Your longest suit is diamonds and the question is how many tricks you can expect to make in it. The easiest way to find the answer is to look and see what high cards are missing. Dummy's suit is missing both ace and king which means that you would expect to lose 2 tricks. But you have the king so that 4 tricks should be made and that is all you need.

You are in a position to win the first trick in either hand but you must be careful to take ♠ Q with ♠ K and leave ♠ A in dummy. This will be what is called an entry card, which means that it represents a means of winning a trick in dummy (in this case) so that you can lead from that hand.

Suppose you were to take the first trick with ♠ A and then started on your diamonds. West might make things difficult by not playing the ◇ A until the third round and this would leave you with no diamond to lead. And with no high card left in dummy to win a trick and get in there would be no hope of playing off the two good diamonds. Therefore play ♠ 3 from dummy and take the opening lead trick in your hand with ♠ K and next lead ◇ K. If this does not bring out the ace, continue until ♢ A appears. Whatever is returned you can win and ♠ A on the table will enable you to carry on with your good suit.

It is important to play ♢ K first. If you were to play ♢ Q and ♢ J it might well happen that you were left with ♢ K and the suit would be blocked. We saw instances of this happening in Hands 2 and 3 of the previous part (page 87).

A sound principle to follow is this. When you suit is solid, first play the high card from the shorter hand. In this case it was possible to establish additional tricks in your long suit by knocking out a high card and it was later possible to get back into the hand with the long suit by using an outside entry card (♠ A).

If you have no entry card outside and the only way into the hand with the suit you are trying to establish is in the suit itself you may have to concede an early trick to your opponents. This is called 'ducking' and an example of ducking by the defenders was given in the previous section. (Hand 4, page 89). Here is an example where the declarer ducks.

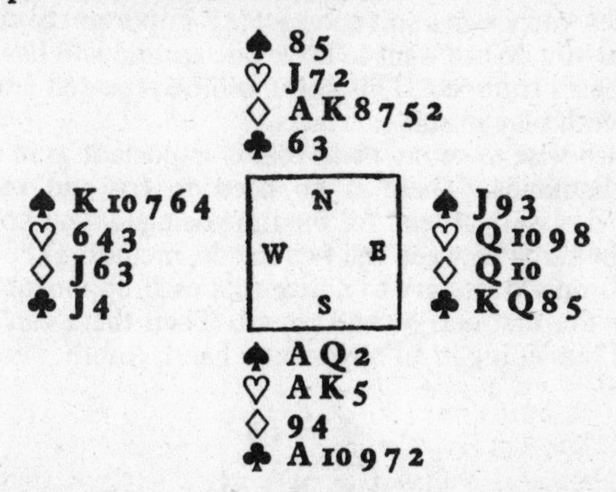

South is declarer in 3 NT and West leads his fourth highest spade (♠ 6) and East's ♠ J is taken with ♠ Q.

Counting the top tricks there are seven (♠ A Q, ♡ A K, ♢ A K and ♣ A) which means that two more must be found. There are two long suits but the diamonds are better than the clubs and you must try to make some of the small cards. The opponents hold between them ♢ Q J 10 and two low cards so there is no way by which you can hope to make all six diamonds. You don't need to anyway, but you can try for five.

If the opposing cards are divided 3 in one hand and 2 in the other (the most likely division) you would find that, after three rounds, the only diamonds left were those in dummy. But if you play out the ace, then the king and then a smaller one, losing, there will not be any way of getting back to dummy.

This is a case where you give the opponents their trick early. After winning the opening lead with ♠ Q you lead ◇ 9 and play ◇ 2 from the table. East wins and returns ♠ 9 (highest card of his partner's lead) and you win this with ♠ A. Now you lead ◇ 4 and take with ◇ K. When each of your opponents follows suit to the second round you can be certain that your four remaining diamonds are winners as the only out-standing card (◇ J) will have to be played on ◇ A. You will make altogether 4 in diamonds, 2 in spades, 2 in hearts and 1 in clubs, scoring an overtrick.

One further point arises from the play of this hand. How necessary is it to try and remember all the cards that have been played and count every suit?

For a start, only try and count suits that are important to you. When you are in a suit contract it is important to count the trumps as you do not want to leave one around and have one of your winners trumped. This point will be repeated later when we deal with play in suit contracts.

It is also wise to count a suit that is important as in the case of the diamonds. There is no need to try and memorize every card played, at least for the time being. If you hold a suit with eight cards between the two hands, including the ace and king, it is only necessary to notice that each opponent has followed to the first and second round. Then there can be only one card remaining in an opponent's hand. Another example –

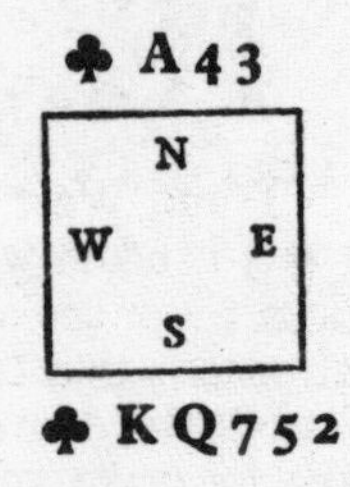

You are South in a no trump contract and you play ♣ A, following with ♣ 2 and then lead ♣ 3 winning with ♣ Q. Providing each opponent follows suit on these two tricks the rest of your clubs are all winners as the only remaining club must be played on your ♣ K. You need not remember which card they played, only that it was a club.

So far we have examined the position where a suit is established to provide additional winners by giving up a trick to the opponents. Sometimes it is possible to avoid letting the opponents' high card take a trick by means of a finesse.

The finesse

The finesse is an attempt to win a trick with a lower card than would be needed to guarantee winning it, hoping that the card that is higher than yours is favourably placed. For example, playing in no trumps –

Needing to make two tricks in diamonds, South leads the ◇ 2 and West plays ◇ 6. By playing ◇ A the trick will certainly be won, but the next round will be taken by the opponents ◇ K. But suppose South plays dummy's ◇ Q, he will win if West holds ◇ K. In other words the play of ◇ Q is an attempt to win the trick with a lower card, hoping that ◇ K is favourably placed, i.e. with the player who has already contributed a low card. It represents an even money chance.

This is the simplest form of finesse. It is possible to extend it where more than one opposing card is involved. e.g.

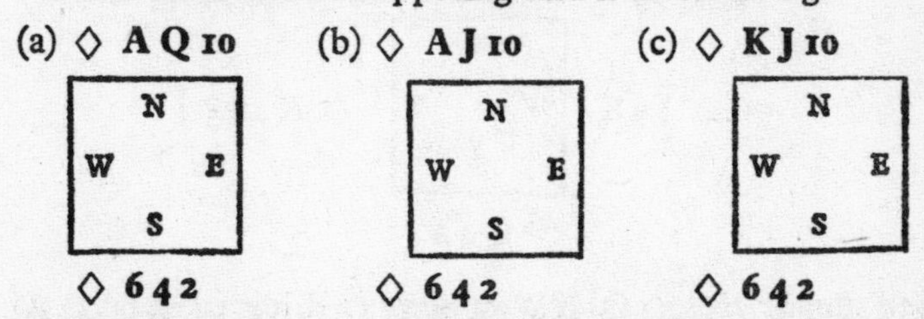

In (a) South leads ◇ 2 and West follows with ◇ 7. If ◇ 10 is played from dummy this offers the possibility of making all three tricks if West holds ◇ K and ◇ J. This would be lucky. But suppose West holds ◇ J, East would have to use ◇ K to win and that would leave ◇ A Q as winners. Alternatively East might take ◇ 10 with ◇ J. South would still have the chance of leading from his hand and playing ◇ Q from dummy. The more complex combination involving three cards has been reduced to a simple finesse such as the one we showed above.

In (b) there is no chance of winning all three tricks and your aim is to win two tricks which will be possible if the king and queen are in different hands. First you lead ◇ 2 and, assuming West plays low, put on ◇ 10 which will probably lose to either ◇ K or ◇ Q. You have now reduced the position to a simple finesse against one card. When you again lead you play ◇ 4 and, if West plays low, you put on ◇ J.

Providing East does not hold both ◇ K and ◇ Q you will take two tricks. In (c) you are hoping for two tricks. You cannot make three as you are missing the ace. The important card is the queen and you must hope that this card is held by West. You lead ◇ 2 and West plays low and you put on ◇ 10. If West holds ◇ Q, East will have to play ◇ A if he wishes to take the trick. By repeating your manoeuvre when you regain the lead you can take two tricks with ◇ J and ◇ K.

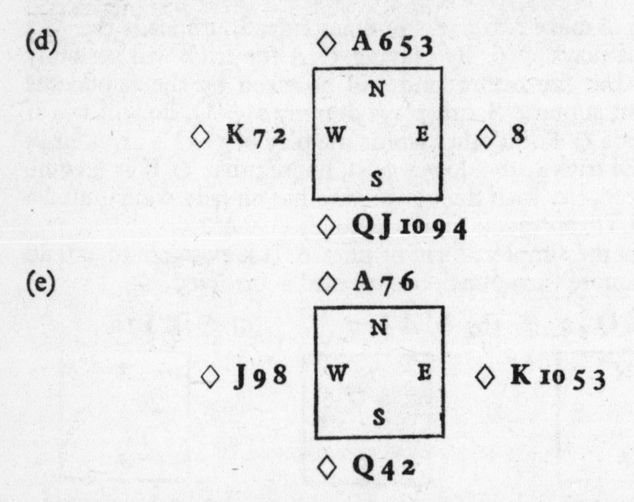

In (d) South leads ◇ Q. If West plays ◇ K it is taken by ◇ A and the remainder of South's cards are winners. If West plays a low card, so also does dummy and ◇ Q wins. South can continue with ◇ J and eventually West's ◇ K is trapped. The reason that South could afford to lead an honour card (◇ Q) was that he had adequate replacements in the event of West playing ◇ K. If ◇ Q, ◇ K and ◇ A all went on the first round ◇ J, 10, 9 would all be elevated to trick taking value. South holds these cards.

In (e) the correct play to try and take two tricks is to lead a low card from dummy towards ◇ Q in the hope that East holds ◇ K. It would be quite wrong to lead ◇ Q towards ◇ A. If West held ◇ K and played it, South would be left with no card capable of winning a trick. Only lead an honour card if you can afford to have it covered.

We have discussed various methods whereby the declarer in a no trump contract can establish additional winners in a long suit by

(1) Forcing out a high card such as an ace.
(2) Giving up an early trick in the suit by ducking.
(3) Trying to avoid a loser by finessing.

These methods all have one thing in common. They involve losing the lead. As we said earlier, in no trump contracts you can only afford to lose the lead according to the number of stoppers you hold in the enemy's suit. In order to keep control you must hold up your stoppers. This feature was mentioned on page 88, Hand 3 in the Defender's Play. Here is a further example.

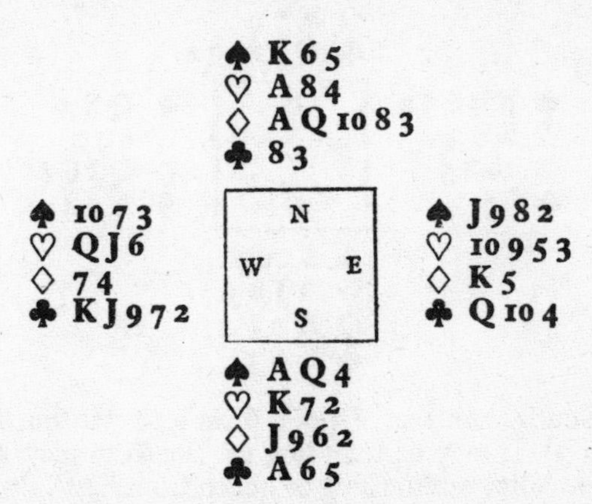

North dealt and opened 1 ◇ and South responded 3 NT – the final contract – holding an evenly distributed 14 points. West led ♣ 7, fourth best of his longest suit, and East as third player played ♣ Q.

South could count seven top tricks (♠ A K Q, ♡ A K, ◇ A and ♣ A) and needed to establish extra tricks in diamonds. Appreciating the danger from the clubs he declined to take either of the first two tricks and won the third, leaving West with two winners in the suit. But West could not get in to play them as he had no card capable of winning a trick. South led ◇ J on which West played ◇ 4 and dummy ◇ 3. This was a finesse against ◇ K. East won but could not return a club as he did not have one. He tried a spade but South was in again and played out the rest of the diamonds and his top cards in spades and hearts, making ten tricks in all.

Had South won the first or second round of clubs, East would have been able to lead back a club when he was in with ◇ K and there would have been no way of preventing West from taking four tricks in clubs. As it was, had East still had a club to play, it would have meant that West only held four to start with and the defenders would win three tricks in clubs.

There is no need to hold up an ace if, by capturing an honour card, you may make a second trick in the suit, as in the following example.

	North	
	♠ J 4 ♡ Q 10 8 ◇ K 7 4 ♣ Q J 10 9 2	
♠ K 9 6 3 2 ♡ K 7 3 ◇ 10 8 5 ♣ 8 7	N W E S	♠ Q 8 5 ♡ 6 4 2 ◇ Q J 6 2 ♣ A 5 4
	♠ A 10 7 ♡ A J 9 5 ◇ A 9 3 ♣ K 6 3	

Against South's contract of 3 NT West leads his fourth highest spade (♠ 3). It may be tempting for South to play ♠ J from the table to 'force out the king or queen from East'. But his own ♠ 10 is just as good as ♠ J and if ♠ 4 is played from dummy, East must play either ♠ Q (or ♠ K) to prevent South winning with ♠ 10.

When East covers dummy's ♠ 4 with ♠ Q it might appear correct from what we have said earlier to play low and keep our ace until later. In that event East will return ♠ 8, highest of partner's lead, and South will win just one trick in spades. But if ♠ Q is taken with ♠ A, South will later take a second trick, for ♠ K will capture ♠ J and ♠ 10 will be a winner on the third round.

So the play will go like this. West leads ♠ 3 covered by ♠ 4, ♠ Q and ♠ A. South can count only four top tricks (♠ A, ♡ A, ◇ A K) but he can increase this number to eight by establishing his clubs. As only one high card is missing, the ace, four out of five of dummy's clubs should take tricks. At trick 2 South leads ♣ K and East wins with ♣ A and returns ♠ 8. West wins with ♠ K and clears his suit by leading another round, which South wins with ♠ 10. South next plays off the rest of his clubs, discarding one heart and one diamond from his hand. West will discard one heart, keeping one low card to protect his king and two diamonds. He must try and keep both his spades.

After playing off the clubs South should make certain of his contract by taking three tricks with ♡ A, ◇ A and ◇ K. It would be bad play to lead ♡ Q from dummy and finesse, playing low from hand in the hope that East held ♡ K, for West would regain the lead and play out two winning spades and defeat the contract.

Your first obligation must be the fulfilment of the contract. Never risk defeat by trying to make an overtrick which is comparatively unimportant.

This hand illustrated the value of the ten when combined with other honours. In these two cases the ten ensures a second trick –

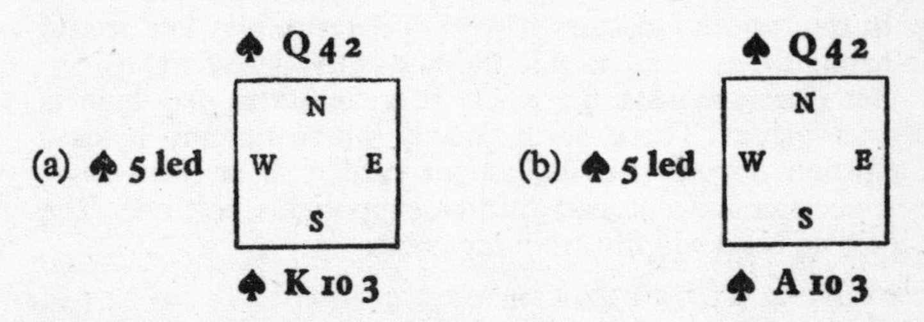

In (a) you play low in dummy and East must play either ♠ A or ♠ J to prevent you winning with ♠ 10. If he plays ♠ A you will make both ♠ K and ♠ Q. If he plays ♠ J, you win with ♠ K. ♠ 10 will take the third round assuming ♠ A has been played on ♠ Q.

Similarly in (b), providing you play low on the first round you will win two tricks by capturing East's ♠ J or ♠ K with ♠ A and subsequently making either ♠ Q or ♠ 10.

Here are two further fairly common honour combinations that deserve a mention as they crop up quite often

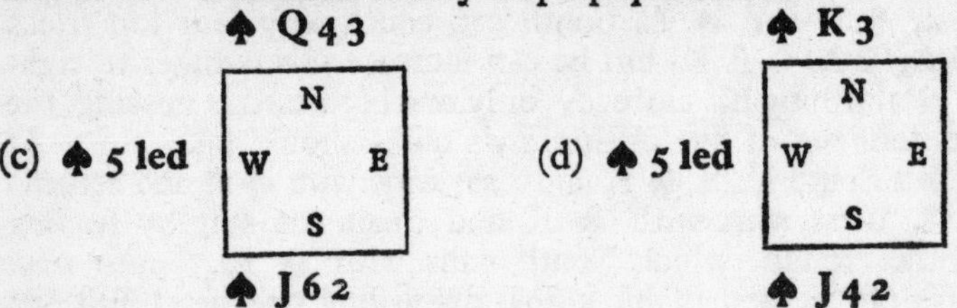

In each case one trick is guaranteed providing you play a low card from dummy on the first round.

In (c) you play ♠ 3 and East must play either ♠ K or ♠ A to prevent you winning with ♠ J. Thus you have drawn out one high card without having used a high card yourself. With ♠ Q and ♠ J remaining you will take a trick. But suppose you had played ♠ Q on the first round and East had won with ♠ A or ♠ K and returned the suit. You are now left with ♠ 4 3 in dummy and ♠ J 6 in your hand and West will probably capture your ♠ J.

Similarly in (d) if you play ♠ 3 and East wins with ♠ Q, your ♠ J will take the third round assuming ♠ A has taken dummy's ♠ K. If you gamble by putting up ♠ K on the first round and it loses to ♠ A, West will probably capture your ♠ J with his ♠ Q.

In the majority of cases it pays declarer to play low second in hand, just as we advised in the case of the defenders.

But there are instances where it is correct to play high as second player. These occur mainly where dummy holds a doubleton honour (i.e. an honour card with one low card) and declarer has no good card to support his best one. The following hand will illustrate the point.

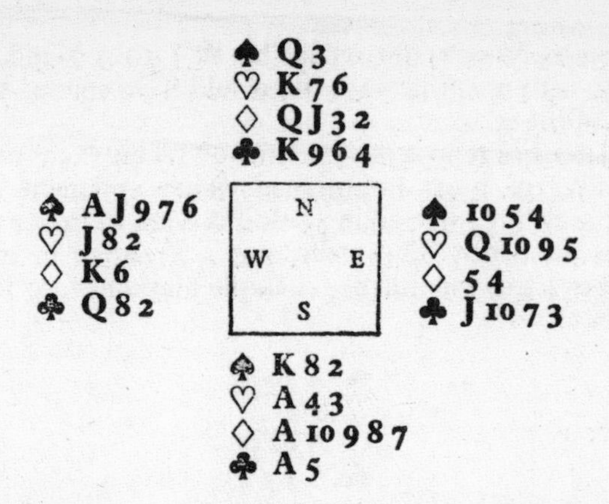

South is declarer in 3 NT after opening 1 ◇ and West overcalling with 1 ♠.

West leads his fourth highest card, ♠ 7, and South's correct play is to put on ♠ Q from the table, He is certain of one trick whatever happens, but if he plays ♠ 3 and East is able to force out his ♠ K, ♠ Q is left unguarded in dummy. Playing ♠ Q at once gives you the chance of winning the trick and still having ♠ K 8 in your hand. (As West bid spades he is likely to hold the ace.)

When ♠ Q wins the next lead should be ◇ Q intending to finesse against ◇ K. If East holds ◇ K you will take all five tricks. As it is West wins the first diamond lead but you are quite safe. If he plays a spade you will win a trick with your ♠ K as you are the last player to play. In other words, if West lays down his ♠ A you can put in ♠ 8 and your ♠ K is now a winner. If West leads a low spade you wait to see what East plays and you either play ♠ K or ♠ 8 depending what is necessary. We will have more to say about the importance of being the last player later.

But before leaving this hand it might be worth pointing out that South could be almost certain that West held ♠ A, apart from the fact that he had bid the suit. In Part 3 on Defence we explained the Rule of Eleven (page 82) and this can be used by the declarer. In the present instance West has led ♠ 7. Deducting 7 from 11 we find that there are four cards higher than the seven, distributed between the remaining three hands. Dummy holds one (♠ Q), South holds two (♠ K 8) so that East holds only one card above the seven. If it were the ace, West's suit would be ♠ J 10 9 7 and, as was explained with opening leads, he would have started with the top card of the sequence, ♠ J not ♠ 7.

If declarer has to lose the lead in a no trump contract it may be a matter of great importance which opponent gets in. Declarer may be protected in a suit if it is led from one side but not from the other. This point was referred to in the hand shown above and this further example may show up the position more clearly.

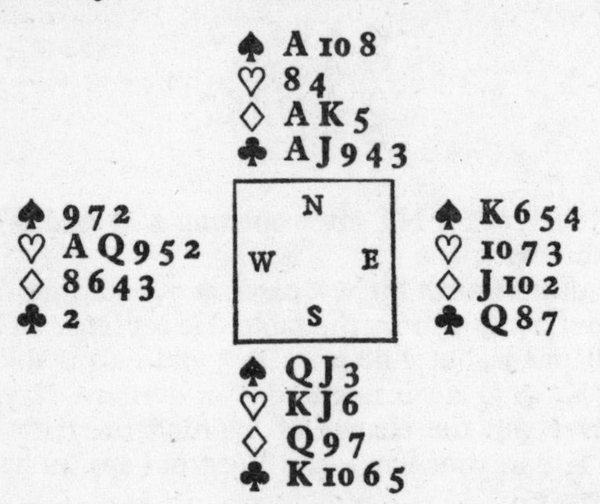

North opens 1 ♣ and South responds 2 NT which is duly raised to 3 NT. West leads ♡ 5 on which East plays ♡ 10 and South wins with ♡ J – leaving him with ♡ K 6. There are, in all, seven top tricks (one spade, one heart, three diamonds and two clubs) and the additional tricks will come from the clubs. Even if a trick is lost to the queen, South will have enough tricks.

With a combined holding of nine cards missing the queen, the usual play is to lay down the ace and king and hope that the queen falls as there are only four cards in the other hands. But South in this case must ask himself 'if I lose the lead and the opponents carry on with their hearts, their best suit, am I certain to regain the lead? East's play of ♡ 10 at trick one makes it almost certain that West holds ♡ A Q. Had East held a higher heart he would have played it as third player. So, if East should get in and lead a heart through South's king, West will make all his remaining hearts because, having seen what card South plays, all he needs to do is to beat it, being careful to play something above dummy's ♡ 8. South must endeavour to prevent East winning a trick. It does not matter if West gets in because if hearts are led from the left up to, as opposed to through, South, the ♡ K is protected because South will be the last player and can decide, when everyone else has played, whether to put on the king or not.

South can achieve his object in this way. At trick 2 he leads ♣ 5 to ♣ A. He must not risk ♣ J as East might (and would) take it. He next returns ♣ 3 and, when East plays ♣ 8, puts on ♣ 10. This means that the trick must be won either by South with ♣ 10 or by West with ♣ Q if he has it. East cannot possibly take the trick. It would be equally correct for South to lead dummy's ♣ J instead of ♣ 3 but East should not play his ♣ Q as he cannot expect to gain by doing so.

In the next example declarer has to keep out the player who has established his long suit.

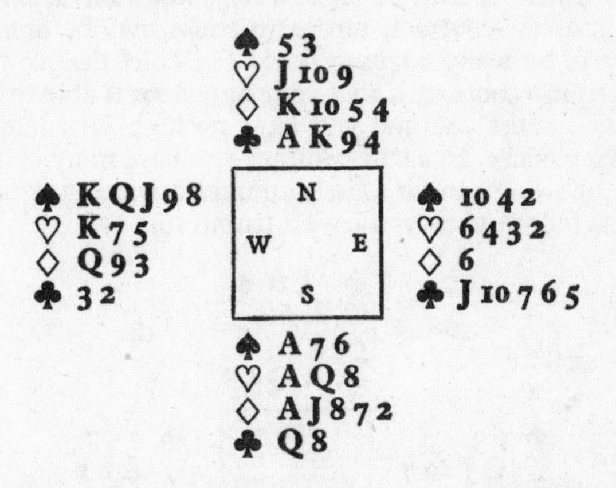

South is declarer in 3 NT having opened 1 ◇ and West overcalling with 1 ♠. West leads ♠ K and South must hold up his ace as he cannot afford to leave himself unprotected in a suit when he cannot be certain of not losing the lead. West continues with ♠ Q which is also allowed to win, and plays a third round forcing out ♠ A.

The position now is that West holds two winning spades. He can only play them out if he takes a trick and thereby gets the lead. South must therefore ensure that, if a trick is lost, it must be East who wins and not West. In order to make nine tricks the diamonds must be established and the queen is missing. South lays down ◇ A from his hand just in case ◇ Q is alone.

He next leads ♢ 2 and covers West's ♢ 9 with ♢ 10 so that the only player who can take the trick is dummy or East. As it happens, dummy's ♢ 10 wins and the play of ♢ K captures West's ♢ Q, and South ends up with ten tricks (1 spade, 1 heart, 5 diamonds and 3 clubs).

Suppose that East had been able to take ♢ 10 with ♢ Q. He had no spade to return to his partner. He would, probably, lead a heart up to weakness on the table. South would have to be careful to play ♡ A in case West won with ♡ K enabling him to lead out his spades. South would make 1 spade, 1 heart, 4 diamonds and 3 clubs for a total of nine tricks. Abbreviated, we can write this 1 ♠, 1 ♡, 4 ♢ and ♣ 3.

B. Suit Contracts

Playing contracts in no trumps, the only way of finding extra tricks is by the establishment of a long suit. A long suit is also useful in a suit contract, but extra tricks may be obtained in other ways by using a trump card. The chief danger you face in a no trump contract is that your opponent is able to set up a long suit against you and you have no high card left to stop him taking tricks. In a suit contract you have more control.

The following hand is a fairly straightforward example of the tactics to follow when you have a trump suit.

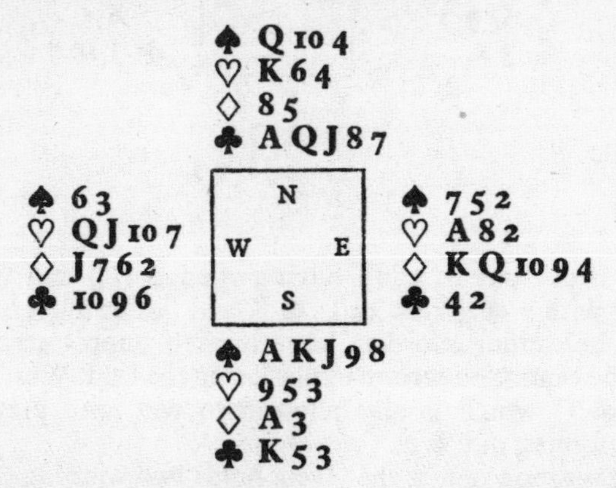

South opens 1 ♠ and North responds 2 ♣, showing at least 8 points and compelling partner to bid again. When South re-bids 2 ♠ North knows he holds more than four so that his holding will be good support. As he could have opened the bidding himself, North supports to game by bidding 4 ♠.

West leads ♡ Q, top of his sequence. There is not much purpose in playing ♡ K so ♡ 4 is played from dummy. East encourages with ♡ 8, West duly continues with ♡ J and the defenders take the first 3 tricks. They will not play a fourth heart because it will be trumped so East, assuming it is now his lead, will play ◇ K, dummy's weakest suit. South must win with ◇ A as he has lost all the tricks he can afford.

If the contract were in no trumps it would not matter whether South played clubs or spades as both are equally solid. But in the present case, if South played clubs next, East would soon have no more and would trump. South must therefore draw trumps, being careful to count how many have been played. When each opponent follows suit twice he knows there is only one more to come. Having pulled the last trump, leaving himself with two, South can safely play clubs. He starts by winning with ♣ K and then leads over to dummy where the length lies. After winning with ♣ A and ♣ Q he plays ♣ J and, having no more clubs left, he is able to discard ◇ 3.

Suppose that South had won the first two club tricks with ♣ A and ♣ Q and the third round with ♣ K, the lead would now be in his hand and he would be unable to get to dummy to play his ♣ J and get rid of his losing diamond.

The importance of being able to get into the right hand is shown in this next example where it is necessary to over-take a winning card.

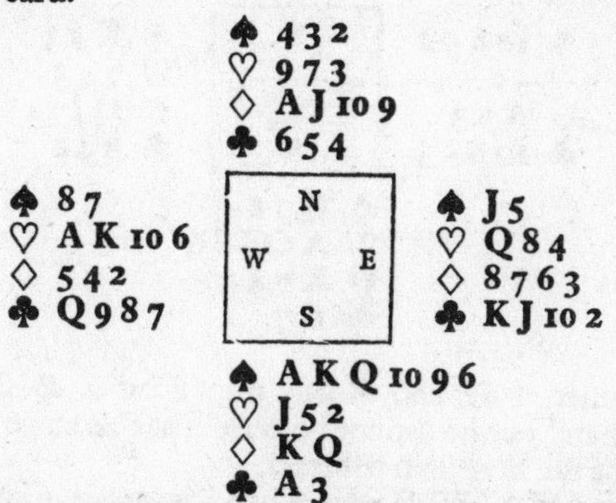

South opened 2 ♠ showing eight playing tricks and a strong suit. With normal distribution he will make all his six spades, together with his ace of clubs and one of his diamonds. As a two bid is normally treated as forcing for one round, North bid 2 NT just to keep the auction open, but promising nothing. South re-bid 3 ♠ and North raised to 4 ♠ on the strength of his diamonds.

West led ♡ A and East encouraged with ♡ 8. West therefore continued with ♡ K and East won the third round with ♡ Q. He then led ♣ J up to dummy's weakness and South won with ♣ A. Two rounds of trumps drew the four shared by the opponents and South had to solve the problem of what to do with his losing club. He saw a way of discarding it on a diamond. He led ◇ K following with ◇ 9 from the table and next led ◇ Q which he overtook with ◇ A. This meant that the lead was in dummy and on ◇ J which was a winner South discarded ♣ 3.

We have emphasized before the importance of studying the hand as soon as dummy goes down, and making a plan. Very often the first trick is vital and a foolish or thoughtless play may be impossible to rectify.

Here is an example where South was lucky enough to hold 30 points between the two hands, but his hasty play to the opening lead resulted in disaster.

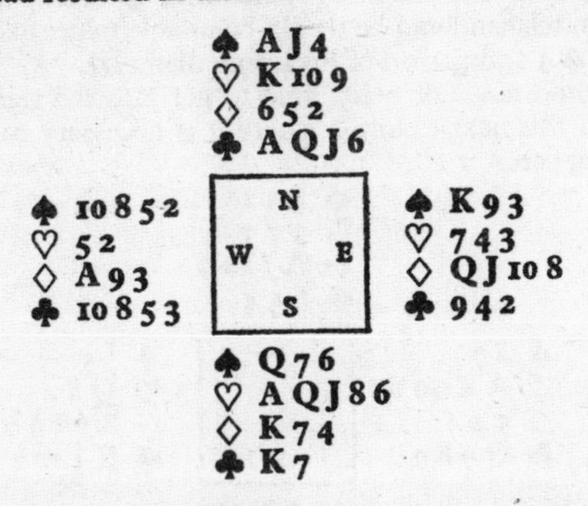

South opened 1 ♡ and North responded 2 ♣. He has an excellent hand but he cannot be certain at this stage which will prove to be the best final contract.

South re-bid 2 NT to give a good impression of all round strength and about 15–16 points in high cards. North next bid 3 ♡ which offered his partner the choice between playing in 3 NT or 4 ♡, depending on whether he held four or five hearts. North could not hold more than three as he would have supported the suit earlier.

South closed the auction with 4 ♡ and West led ♠ 2. Without stopping to think, South played ♠ 4 from dummy hoping to win the first trick with ♠ Q.

But East played ♠ K and, seeing no point in leading back into the strength, returned ◇ Q to the weakness on the table. This proved to be a fatal blow to South, whose ◇ K was captured with ◇ A and he found himself losing the first four tricks for one down (contract defeated by one trick). South should have counted his tricks. He has five tricks in trumps as all the top cards are shared between himself and dummy. He has four tricks in clubs and one in spades. He may well make a second spade and may possibly make a diamond, but at least he is in a position to win the first ten tricks for his contract. Therefore he should have put up ♠ A and then drawn trumps. He next plays ♣ K and follows with ♣ 7 (high card first from the short hand) and plays off his winners, discarding ◇ 7 4 from his hand.

Having taken the first 8 tricks and still holding 2 trumps he cannot go down.

He can now afford to lead a spade. East wins with ♠ K and leads a diamond, ◇ K being taken with ◇ A. But South takes the remaining tricks with 2 trumps and ♠ Q, making an overtrick.

A similar disaster occurred on this hand.

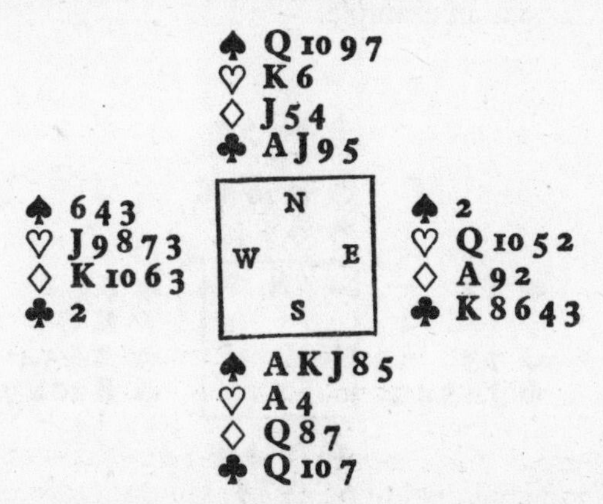

South opened 1 ♠ and bid game after a reply of 3 ♠. West led ♣ 2 and South played ♣ 5 and lost to East's ♣ K. East could guess that his partner had led a singleton. Had it been fourth best South would not have had a club at all. If West had held two clubs (doubleton) he would have led the higher.

So East returned the suit and West trumped. West guessed right and returned a diamond which East won with ◇ A and led back another club. Including ◇ K the defenders took the first five tricks beating South's contract by two tricks.

South's reasoning should be on these lines. There are 5 winners in trumps and 2 in hearts. It should be quite possible to make 3 tricks in clubs as only the king need win a trick for the opponents. Providing diamonds are not played initially by declarer only 2 tricks need be lost.

In other words 2 diamonds and 1 club are the only losers. Therefore do not take unnecessary risks; put up ♣ A and get in early and draw trumps. Having drawn trumps lead ♣ Q and force out ♣ K. If East leads back a low diamond be careful to play low second in hand to make sure of one trick.

South can afford to play ♣ A at trick one because he has only 3 apparent losers. But if his diamonds were 9 8 7 (not Q 8 7) he would have to take a chance on winning the opening lead with ♣ Q. Because with 3 losing diamonds he cannot afford to give away a club. It is his only chance.

But with ◇ Q 8 7 he has only 2 losing diamonds and there is absolutely no point in taking a gamble on the position of ♣ K.

The last hand introduced the subject of counting losers. In suit contracts it is advisable to count up the losers as well as the winners. Here is an example:

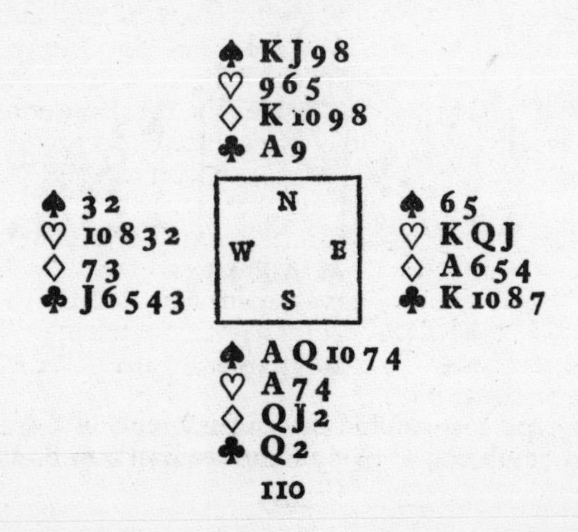

South is declarer in 4 ♠ and West leads ♣ 4. Counting winners you have 5 spades, 1 heart, 1 club for certain and you expect to establish 3 diamonds after forcing out ◇ A. That comes to ten tricks. What can you lose? Certainly 1 diamond, possibly 1 club and maybe 2 hearts. In other words you have 10 winners but possibly 4 losers. You plan to discard one loser on the fourth diamond but it is important that you should be able to drive out the ◇ A before the enemy drive out your ♡ A.

This is the critical point of the hand and again demonstrates the essential need to consider the situation before playing to the first trick.

You must win the first trick with ♣ A and then draw trumps, leaving one high one in dummy in case you need an entry card. After drawing trumps you lead ◇ Q and continue with the suit until ◇ A has been played. East, after winning with ◇ A can play his ♣ K and then lead ♡ K. You will regain the lead with ♡ A and carry on with your diamonds, discarding a heart on the fourth diamond.

Consider what would have happened if you had played the low club from the table at trick one. East would win with ♣ K and attack dummy's weakness by leading ♡ K. You would have to part with your ace. When later, you sought to establish your diamonds East would get in with ◇ A and play out 2 winning hearts. Failure to play ♣ A at trick one has left you a move behind.

The three last examples have all had one thing in common. Declarer has been offered a finesse on the first round. In all such cases you should ask yourself two questions. Firstly, is the finesse necessary? Secondly, if it is taken and fails, is the contract in danger? In all three cases the finesse was not necessary. In all three cases it was dangerous to risk the finesse.

In all the hands quoted in this section the declarer has drawn trumps as soon as possible. This policy is correct in most instances where there are winners in other suits to play off and the trump suit is sufficiently strong. It is a bad mistake to start playing out a good suit and allow your opponent to trump. There is a saying in England that many a man walks London's River Thames Embankment, homeless, because he forgot to draw the trumps. Probably a similarly unhappy future is predicted for those in America and other parts of the world who also fail to draw trumps.

But the population on the Embankment is cosmopolitan and there are almost as many there because they drew trumps as there are because they didn't. In other words, there are circumstances where it is wrong to play trumps at once.

A common instance is where dummy is short in a suit and one or more of declarer's losers can be ruffed (i.e. trumped). For example –

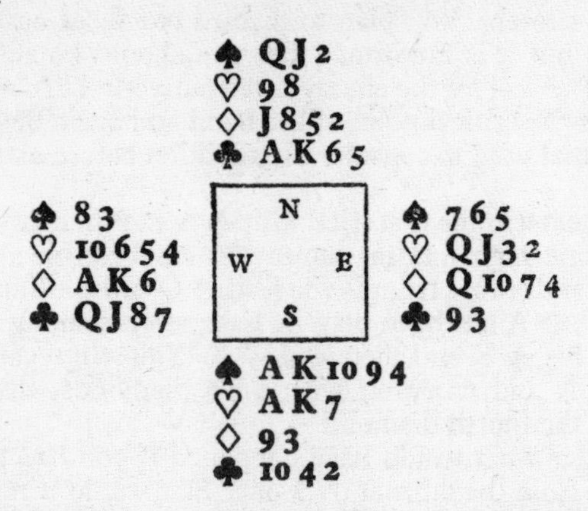

South is declarer in 4 ♠ and West leads ◇ A and is encouraged by East's ◇ 7. He continues with ◇ K and ◇ 6 and South ruffs the third round with ♠ 4.

South can count on making 5 spades, including the one he has used, 2 hearts and 2 clubs – total 9. He might hope for another trick in clubs if each opponent holds 3 but this would be very lucky. He can trump another diamond in his hand but this would not give him an extra trick as he has already counted on making 5 tricks in spades. Consider the hearts. If South plays off his ♡ A K dummy will then have no heart. South can then lead his ♡ 7, a loser, and take it with a trump in dummy. This will mean that he has made a trump trick on the table without having had to play a trump from his own hand. After ruffing ♡ 7 trumps can be drawn.

The extra trick would not have been made if South had drawn trumps at once as dummy's three trump cards would have all fallen on South's.

In the next example it is necessary to give up a trick before using one of dummy's trumps.

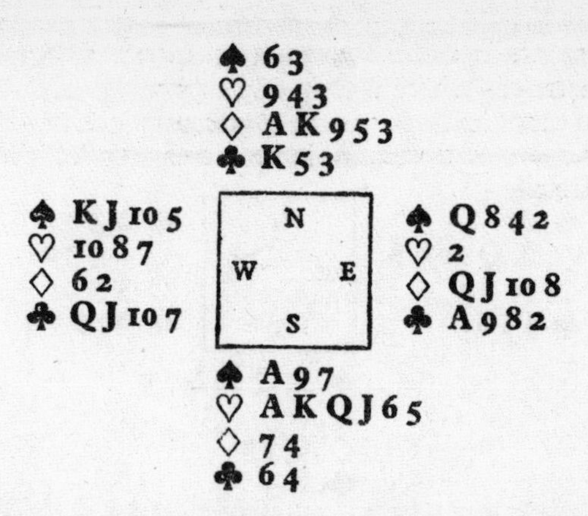

South opened 1 ♡ and North responded 2 ◇. South made a jump re-bid of 3 ♡ to indicate 7 probable winners in his own hand including a good suit, and North raised to 4 ♡.

West led ♣ Q, top of a sequence, and the defence took the first two tricks; South trumped the third round. Here again the value of a trump suit is shown, for otherwise there would be no way of preventing the loss of at least 4 tricks in clubs.

South can see only nine tricks (6 hearts, 2 diamonds and 1 spade). He would need a lot of luck to make an extra diamond but he can make use of the fact that dummy holds only 2 spades. After winning the third trick he leads ♠ A and then ♠ 7. West wins but South must regain the lead at the next trick. He now plays ♠ 9 and trumps in dummy. He thus makes an extra trick. Had he played out his trumps at once dummy's three would have fallen on his own.

Supposing that he had played two rounds only and then played his spades, West would win and, seeing what declarer was hoping to do would play his ♡ 10, removing the last trump from the table.

Another situation in which it is wrong to draw trumps at once is where there is a necessity to discard a loser quickly. Consider this example.

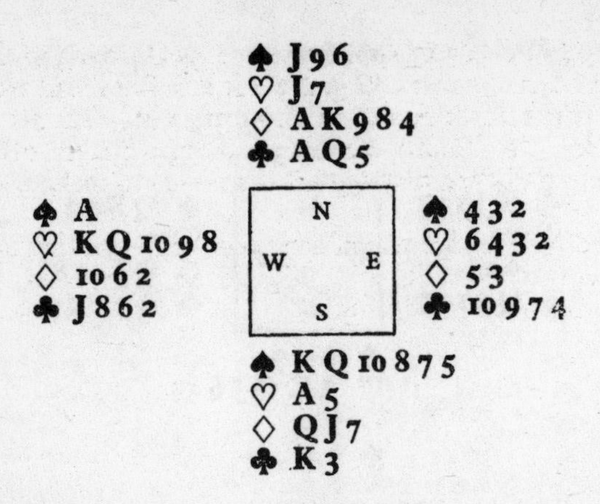

North deals and opens 1 ◇. South makes a game forcing bid of 2 ♠ having 15 points and a good suit. North re-bids 3 ◇ to show at least five and South repeats his spades (3 ♠) to confirm length. His alternative bid is 4 ◇. North can now raise to 4 ♠. Once he has received some support for his suit, South can try for a slam and uses the Blackwood Convention, bidding 4 NT to ask about aces. North responds 5 ♡ to show 2 aces. South cannot be certain which these are but if the ace of clubs is missing the suit will be protected if the lead comes from the left so South bids 6 ♠.

West leads ♡ K which South wins with ♡ A. Counting up the winning tricks, there are 5 in spades, 1 in hearts, 4 (probably 5) in diamonds and 3 in clubs. That makes 13 tricks which means a grand slam.

But what about the losers? South is missing the ace of trumps and nothing can prevent that trick being lost. Also the lead of ♡ K has forced out ♡ A and left South with a losing heart in each hand. If he leads trumps at this point the opponents will take the trick with ♠ A and immediately play ♡ Q to defeat the contract.

Before leading a spade South must look for a way of discarding his losing heart. He must look for a suit where he has more cards in one hand than the other.

There are two such suits, diamonds and clubs. It would be impossible to play diamonds three times without someone trumping but the clubs are much safer. The opponents hold 8 cards between them in clubs and it is unlikely that one player has only two and his partner six. Therefore South plays

♣ K followed by ♣ 3 to ♣ A and leads ♣ Q. Being unable to follow suit he can discard ♡ 5. Now it is safe to lead trumps. West will win with ♠ A and will doubtless play out his ♡ Q. but he is too late. South can trump. South merely needs to draw trumps and then play out his diamonds to make his slam contract.

The need to take care which opponent gains the lead applies to suit contracts equally as it does to no trumps explained earlier on page 104. For example –

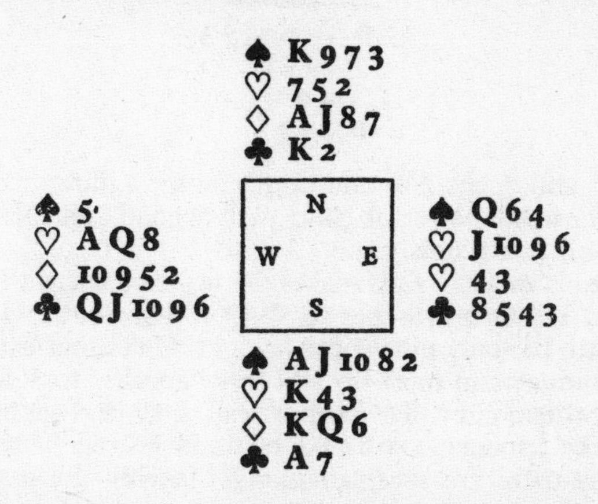

South is declarer in 4 ♠ and West leads ♣ Q. South can count 4 tricks in diamonds, 2 in clubs, and if he makes 4 out of his 5 tricks in spades he will have enough. But he might lose 3 hearts and 1 spade. If his opponents get in they will probably attack hearts and a heart lead from East on the right through the king will be much more embarrassing than a lead from West up to the king.

South must therefore keep East out of the lead by playing ♠ K and then ♠ 3, finessing ♠ 10 when East follows with ♠ 6. If West holds ♠ Q South is in no danger.

Whenever you hold a king without either the ace or queen in either hand to balance it, try and make sure that you, with the king, will be the last hand to play if the suit is led.

Playing in a suit contract may enable you to establish a long suit in which high cards are missing without giving away a trick. This is done by ruffing out the suit. By trumping the opponents' winners you reach a point when the cards you hold are the only ones left. Here is an example –

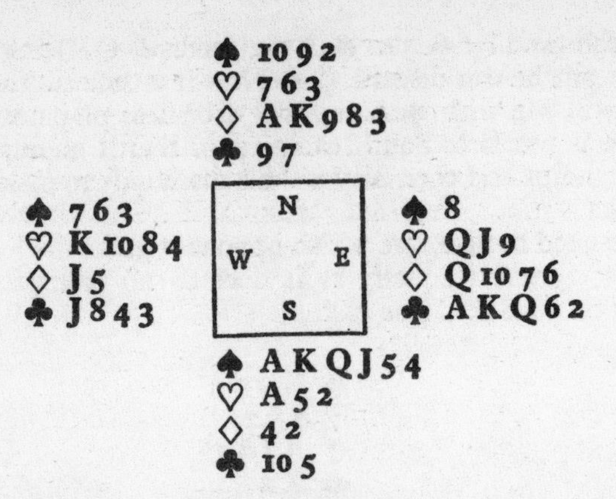

East deals and opens 1 ♣ and South makes a jump overcall of 2 ♠ to show his powerful hand with a good suit. North can support and South bids game.

West leads ♣ 3 and East makes the first two tricks with ♣ Q and ♣ A. He then switches to ♡ Q which South wins with ♡ A. South has only nine tricks in sight. He cannot trump any loser in dummy and must try and make another trick from his long suit (diamonds). He cannot lead a ♡ and give a trick away as the opponents will take tricks in hearts. Between the two hands there are seven diamonds, leaving the opponents with six. These are most likely to divide 4–2 or 3–3. That is to say one opponent will hold four and his partner two, or they might be evenly split. Provided that neither opponent holds more than four, dummy's last diamond can be made into a winner, for after four rounds there will be none left.

After playing out ♠ A South leads a diamond and wins 2 tricks with ♢ A and ♢ K, each opponent following suit. He next leads ♢ 3 on which East plays ♢ 10 and South trumps with ♠ K. This is necessary to avoid West over-trumping and also because South must retain some small trumps to lead over to dummy.

Dummy is entered by leading ♠ 4 to ♠ 9 and ♢ 8 is led, East playing ♢ Q and South trumping with ♠ Q. This is the fourth round of diamonds and ♢ 9 on the table is the only one left and therefore a winner. It is possible to lead over to the table with ♠ 5 taken by ♠ 10 and one of South's losing hearts is discarded on the winning diamond.

It would have been impossible to establish the diamonds in this way in no trumps. As it was it could only be achieved because South held very strong trumps and could afford to keep using them and still be able to draw those in the opposing hands. Using high trumps enabled South to get back to dummy.

When you hold solid trumps (as here) it is correct to ruff with medium sized ones (not the lowest). After all, when all the trumps are out, any that remain will be tricks whether they are ace and king or the two and three.

Declarer's Play Quiz

1. In each of the following you are East, declarer in 3 NT with no opposition bidding.

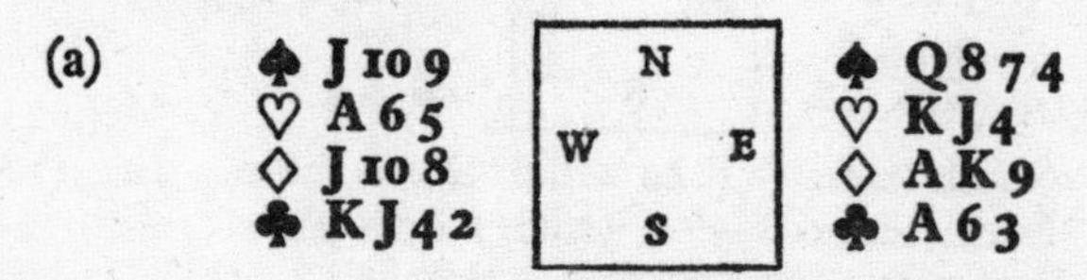

South leads ♡ 7

(i) How many top tricks do you have?
(ii) In which hand will the first trick be won?
(iii) How do you plan to make the contract?

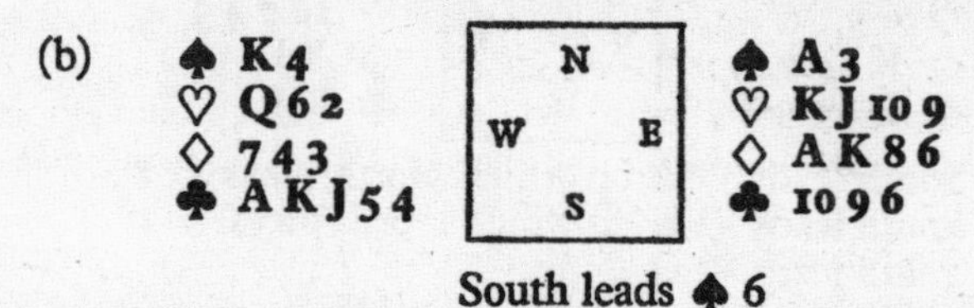

South leads ♠ 6

(i) How many top tricks do you have?
(ii) How do you plan to make the contract?

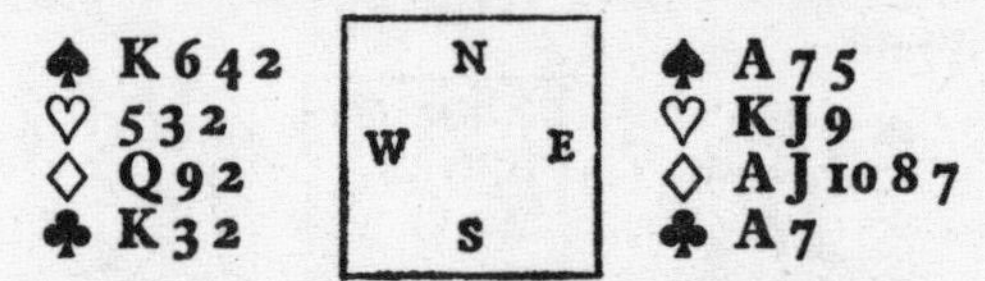

South leads ♡ 7 and North plays ♡ Q.

(i) How many top tricks do you have?
(ii) How do you plan to make the contract?

(d)

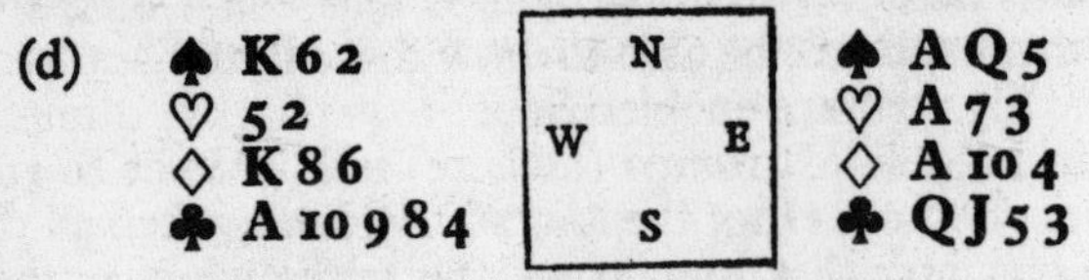

South leads ♡ 6 and North plays ♡ K.

(i) How many top tricks do you have?
(ii) How do you plan to make the contract?

2. You are East, declarer in 4 ♡ with no opposition bidding.

(a)

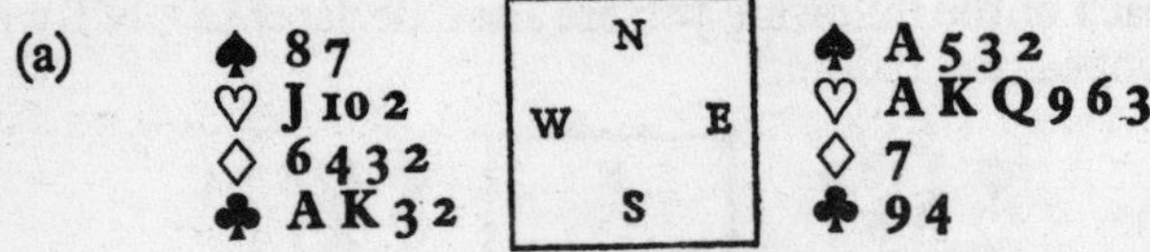

South leads ◇ K to which North follows with ◇ 8
South leads ◇ 5 on which North plays ◇ A.

(i) How many top tricks do you have?
(ii) How do you plan to make the contract?

(b) You are East, declarer in 4 ♠. South overcalled your opening bid of 1 ♠ with 2 ♡.

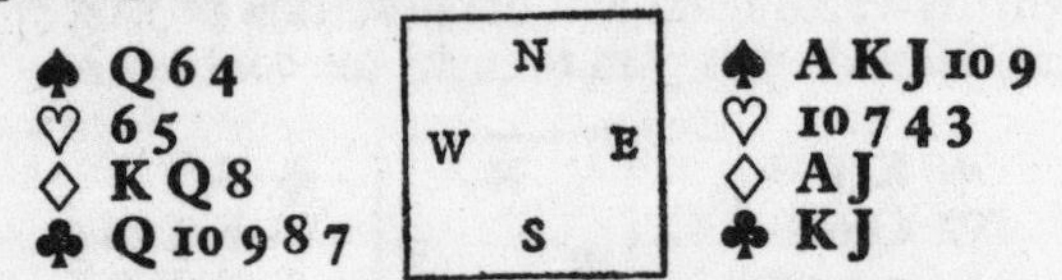

South leads ♡ A on which North plays ♡ 8
South leads ♡ K on which North plays ♡ 2
South leads ♡ Q.

(i) What card to you play from dummy on trick 3?
(ii) How do you plan to make your contract?

(c) You are East, declarer in 6 ♠ with no opposition bidding.

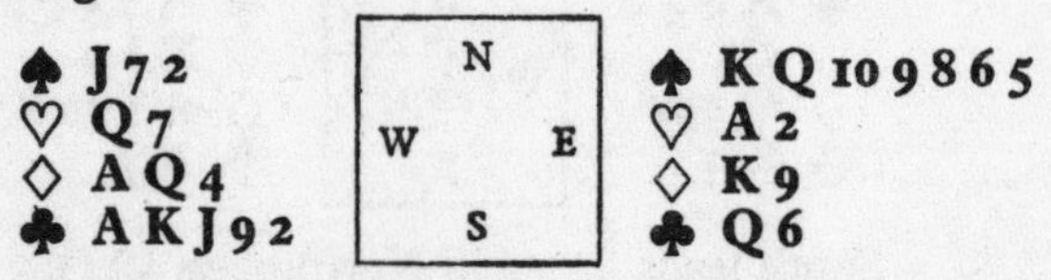

South leads ♡ J which is covered by dummy's ♡ Q and North plays ♡ K.
How do you plan to make your contract?

(d) You are East, declarer in 4 ♠. You opened 3 ♠ (pre-emptive bid) and the opponents did not bid.

South leads ♡ Q.

(i) Should you win the first trick?
(ii) How do you plan to make your contract?

Answers to the Part Three Declarer's Play Quiz follow on the next page.

Answers to Declarer's Play Quiz

1. (a) (i) 7 top tricks. As a heart has been led and you hold ♡ K J 4 you must take 3 tricks. If North plays ♡ Q you take with ♡ K and still have ♡ A and ♡ J between you. If North plays ♡ 10 or lower you win with ♡ J and still have ♡ A and ♡ K. In addition you hold ◇ A K and ♣ A and ♣ K.
(ii) In your hand with either ♡ K or ♡ J.
(iii) Play spades, forcing out ♠ A and ♠ K while you have all suits stopped. You will thus win 2 extra tricks in spades.

(b) (i) 6 top tricks. (♠ A K, ◇ A K and ♣ A K).
(ii) Play hearts at once to make 3 tricks to add to your other 6. You have already counted on making ♣ A K so you would only make 3 extra tricks in clubs if you were lucky and captured ♣ Q.

(c) (i) 6 top tricks. (♠ A K, ♡ K (as the suit has been led) ◇ A and ♣ AK).
(ii) Win with ♡ K. Enter dummy with either ♠ K or ♣ K and lead ◇ Q or ◇ 9 and finesse. If South holds ◇ K and continues hearts, you are protected with ♡ J 9.

(d) (i) 7 top tricks. (♠ A K Q, ♡ A, ◇ A K and ♣ A).
(ii) Hold up ♡ A until third round. Lead ♣ Q and finesse, hoping South holds ♣ K. If North wins with ♣ K he probably has no heart to return. If he does have a heart the suit is probably divided 4–4 between North–South.

2. (a) (i) 9 top tricks. (1 in spades, 6 in hearts and 2 in clubs).
(ii) Trump the second diamond and lead ♠ A and ♠ 2 in order to trump low spades in dummy. By trumping 2 spades you should make 11 tricks in all.

(b) (i) ♠ Q. North has played high–low and will also be able to trump. This is consistent with the fact that South overcalled and will hold 5 hearts. As your trumps are solid you can well afford ♠ Q.
(ii) Draw trumps and lead ◇ A followed by ◇ J and discard ♡ 10 on ◇ K. Next play a club, You must discard your ♡ 10 before playing a club for otherwise South will win with ♣ A and play ♡ J.

(c) Win with ♡ A and play ◇ K followed by ◇ 9 and discard ♡ 2 on dummy's third diamond. This must be done before leading trumps.

(d) (i) Win with ♡ A. If you allow ♡ Q to win opponents may attack clubs.

(ii) Lead a diamond at trick 2 to force out ◇ A so that you can discard a club on ◇ K. You have 4 losers, one in each suit. You cannot prevent the loss of a spade and diamond as you are missing the ace and the heart lead has driven out your ♡ A. But you need not lose a club if you can discard it in time.

SCORING TABLE

(*As published in the authorised edition of the Laws of Contract Bridge 1993, by kind permission*)

TRICK SCORE

Scored *below the line* by *declarer's side,* if contract is fulfilled.

	IF TRUMPS ARE			
For each trick over six bid and made	♣	♦	♥	♠
undoubled	20	20	30	30
doubled	40	40	60	60
redoubled	80	80	120	120

	AT A NO-TRUMP-CONTRACT		
	Undoubled	Doubled	Redoubled
For the first trick over six, bid and made	40	80	160
For each additional trick over six, bid and made	30	60	120

The first side to score 100 points below the line, in one or more hands, win a GAME. When a game is won, both sides start without trick score toward the next game. First side to win two games wins the RUBBER points.

PREMIUM SCORE

Scored *above the line* by *declarer's side:*

SLAMS

For making a SLAM	Not vulnerable	Vulnerable
Small Slam (12 tricks) bid and made	500	750
Grand Slam (all 13 tricks) bid and made	1000	1500

OVERTRICKS

For each OVERTRICK (tricks made in excess of contract)	Not vulnerable	Vulnerable
undoubled	Trick value	Trick value
doubled	100	200
redoubled	200	400
For making any doubled contract	50	50
For making any redoubled contract	100	100

RUBBER, GAME, PART-SCORE

For winning RUBBER, if opponents have won no game 700
For winning RUBBER, if opponents have won one game 500
UNFINISHED RUBBER – for having won one game 300
UNFINISHED RUBBER – for having the only part-score (or scores) 50

HONOURS

Scored *above the line by either side:*

For holding four of the five trump HONOURS (A, K, Q, J, 10) in one hand 100
For holding all five trump HONOURS (A, K, Q, J, 10) in one hand 150
For holding all four ACES in one hand at a no-trump contract 150

UNDERTRICK PENALTIES

Scored *above the line* by declarer's *opponents* if contract is *not fulfilled:*

UNDERTRICKS

(tricks by which declarer fails to fulfil the contract)

	Not Vulnerable			Vulnerable		
	Und'bled	Doubled	Red'bled	Und'bled	Doubled	Red'bled
For first under-trick	50	100	200	100	200	400
For each additional under-trick	50	200	400	100	300	600

GLOSSARY OF BRIDGE TERMS

AUCTION. The series of bids made by the players to determine the number of tricks to be won either with a trump suit or with no trumps. (See page 13).

BALANCED HAND. Evenly distributed. (See page 21).

BID. An undertaking to win at least a specified number of tricks over and above six, either with a suit as trumps or with no trumps. (See page 9.)

BIDDABLE SUIT. A suit that is considered strong enough to bid, which will in most cases comprise at least four cards. (See page 23).

BLOCKING. A situation in which the high cards in one hand, unaccompanied by low cards, prevent playing winners in the same suit from the opposite hand. (See page 87).

BUSINESS DOUBLE. A double suggesting that the contract will fail. Also termed Penalty Double. (See page 11).

CONTRACT. The undertaking by declarer's side to win a specified number of tricks over and above six, either with a suit as trumps or with no trumps. This definition is similar to that of a bid but a bid may be followed by a higher bid. It is the highest bid that represents the contract. The essence of bidding for the contract gives the game its name – Contract Bridge. (See page 9).

CONVENTION. A call or play which, by partnership agreement, carries a special message. (See page 38).

CUE BID. A forcing bid in a suit in which the bidder cannot reasonably wish to play, to convey to partner that he can win the first or second round (rarely the third) if the suit is led. (See page 60).

CUT. Drawing cards to determine the partnership. (See page 12).

DECLARER. The player who plays the hand. (See page 14).

DEFENDERS. The two players who are trying to prevent the declarer making the number of tricks he has undertaken to win. (See page 14).

DEFENSIVE TRICK. A trick that is likely to be made even though the opponents are playing the hand. (See page 22).

DISCARD. To throw away a non-trump card when unable to follow suit. (See page 74).

DOUBLETON. A suit containing two cards. (See page 24).

DUMMY. Declarer's partner. (See page 14).

ENTRY CARD. A card that enables a player to win a trick to permit him to lead from a particular hand. (See page 94).

FINESSE. An attempt to win a trick with a lower card than the one that would be sure to win. (See page 97).

FOLLOW SUIT. Playing a card of the same suit that was led. (See page 7).

FORCING. A bid that demands that partner should reply either at least once (forcing one round) or until a game contract has been reached (forcing to game). (See page 23).

GAME. A score below the line amounting to at least 100 points. (See page 10).

HONOURS. The Ace, King, Queen, Knave (or Jack), Ten. (See page 12).

LIMIT BID. A bid that conveys the value of the hand within a narrow range of strength. (See page 31).

MAKE. To shuffle. (See page 12).

MAJOR SUIT. The higher ranking suits – spades and hearts (See page 10).

MINOR SUITS. The lower ranking suits – diamonds and clubs. (See page 10).

NO TRUMPS. Playing without having any suit as trumps. (See page 9).

OVERTRICKS. Tricks made in excess of what you have contracted to win. (See page 78).

OVERTRUMP. To trump with a higher trump than the previous player.

PART SCORE. A trick score below the line, less than 100. (See page 10).

PASS. No Bid. (See page 13).

PENALTY DOUBLE. Also called business double. A call by a player implying that the opponent's contract will be defeated. The effect of the double is to increase the penalty if the contract fails. If the contract *is* made the trick score is doubled and a bonus of 50 points above the line is awarded.

PLAYING TRICKS. Tricks that you are likely to win if you play the contract in your selected denomination.

PRE-EMPTIVE BID. A high barrage bid. (See page 57).

QUICK TRICKS. Card or combinations of cards that will win a trick on the first or second round. (See page 71).

RE-BID. The second and subsequent bid made by a player. (See page 45).

RESPONDER. The player who replies to a bid made by the partner. (See page 23).

REVOKE. Failure to follow suit when able to do so. (See page 7).

RUBBER. The side which first wins two games is said to have won the rubber and is credited with bonus points. (See page 9).

RUFF. To trump. (See page 9).

SINGLETON. A suit containing one card in the suit (See page 37).

SIGN OFF. To indicate by a bid an unwillingness for partner to bid any further. (See page 40).

SLAM. A contract to win either twelve tricks (Little Slam) or thirteen tricks (Grand Slam). (See page 12).

STOPPER. A card or combination of cards that will win a trick. (See page 93).

TAKE OUT DOUBLE. A double by a player asking partner to call his best suit. Also referred to as Informatory Double. (See page 62).

THROWN IN. When all four players say 'no bid', the hand is thrown in and no points are scored. The deal passes in the normal way.

TOP TRICKS. Tricks that can be won without conceding the lead. (See page 93).

TRICK. A group of four cards, one contributed by each player in rotation. (See page 8).

TRUMP. Each card of a suit that represents the final contract. The trump card has priority over other suits for trick taking purposes. (See page 8).

UNDERTRICKS. Each trick by which the declarer's side fails to make the contract. (See page 17).

VULNERABLE. The term applied to a side that has scored a game. The effect of being vulnerable is that penalties for undertricks are greater, as also are the premiums for certain achievements, e.g. slams. (See page 18).

VOID. Holding no cards in a suit.

Also available

THE RIGHT WAY TO PLAY BRIDGE

This book is for those who want to improve their bridge at a social, or competitive, level. Clear examples expose the detail of modern Acol bidding. From these you learn to plan and reassess your campaign step-by-step and calculate with precision who holds which cards. You also discover when to obstruct with bluff and bombast, how to pinpoint best leads and steal the best contracts, and ways to think strategically under pressure.

Unique at-the-table charts – designed to foster partnership understanding used appropriately at home, club or class – summarise key bids.

The author, Paul Mendelson, is a bridge professional at the Roehampton Club and teaches throughout London. He is a keen tournament competitor, having been National Schools' champion, as well as the youngest ever captain of a winning Devonshire Cup team.

BEGIN BACKGAMMON

This is a complete introduction for the novice. Backgammon is characterised by a unique combination of skill and chance. Success depends on understanding the arithmetical probabilities which underlie the throw of two dice. Author, Vere Molyneux, explains these probabilities in a way that the newest beginner will understand. Besides probabilities, much attention is given to strategy, gambling and doubling, and the beginner is run through an excellent sample game with commentary.

CARD GAMES PROPERLY EXPLAINED

Develop 'card sense' with Arnold Marks. Find out how to play the right card at the right moment. Not only does the author clearly explain the rules of each game, but he also shows how to develop your skill to win the game. Covers Whist, Solo, Napoleon, Clobbiosh, Belot, Poker and much more.

PICK OF THE PACK PATIENCE GAMES

Here Jacqueline Harrod describes one hundred of the best Patience games, ranging from very simple ones which will keep children happy to the most complex ones which demand utmost clarity of thought from intelligent adults!

RIGHT WAY
PUBLISHING POLICY

HOW WE SELECT TITLES

RIGHT WAY consider carefully every deserving manuscript. Where an author is an authority on his subject but an inexperienced writer, we provide first-class editorial help. The standards we set make sure that every **RIGHT WAY** book is practical, easy to understand, concise, informative and delightful to read. Our specialist artists are skilled at creating simple illustrations which augment the text wherever necessary.

CONSISTENT QUALITY

At every reprint our books are updated where appropriate, giving our authors the opportunity to include new information.

FAST DELIVERY

We sell **RIGHT WAY** books to the best bookshops throughout the world. It may be that your bookseller has run out of stock of a particular title. If so, he can order more from us at any time – we have a fine reputation for "same day" despatch, and we supply any order, however small (even a single copy), to any bookseller who has an account with us. We prefer you to buy from your bookseller, as this reminds him of the strong underlying public demand for **RIGHT WAY** books. Readers who live in remote places, or who are housebound, or whose local bookseller is unco-operative, can order direct from us by post.

FREE

If you would like an up-to-date list of all **RIGHT WAY** titles currently available, please send a stamped self-addressed envelope to

ELLIOT RIGHT WAY BOOKS,
KINGSWOOD, SURREY, KT20 6TD, U.K.